THE THEATRICAL MANAGER IN
ENGLAND AND AMERICA

The Theatrical Manager in England and America

PLAYER OF A PERILOUS GAME

Philip Henslowe   *Tate Wilkinson*

Stephen Price

Edwin Booth   *Charles Wyndham*

EDITED BY JOSEPH W. DONOHUE, JR.

PRINCETON UNIVERSITY PRESS 1971

PRINCETON, NEW JERSEY

Publication of this book has been aided by the
Annan Fund of the Department of English,
Princeton University

This book has been composed in Linotype Baskerville
Printed in the United States of America
by Princeton University Press, Princeton, New Jersey

124938

Foreword

THE ESSAYS collected in this volume were originally delivered as lectures at Princeton University during the course of the 1969-70 academic year. They were arranged in honor of Gerald Eades Bentley, then Murray Professor of English Literature, in the year of his retirement from the Princeton faculty. In order to pay tribute to Professor Bentley's lifetime of scholarship on the theatre, principally embodied in his seven-volume work *The Jacobean and Caroline Stage* (Oxford, 1941-68), his colleague Professor Alan S. Downer conceived the idea of a series of lectures on a subject central to theatrical scholarship but in great need of extensive consideration: the role of the theatrical manager.

In the broadside announcing the series, sponsored by the Department of English at Princeton and collectively entitled "Players of a Perilous Game," Professor Downer explained the importance of the subject:

> From Philip Henslowe to David Merrick, the producer or theatre manager has generally been seen as a combination of Shylock and Simon Legree, usurer and slave-driver, wholly concerned with profit and loss, indifferent to art and artists. Yet no single person has greater responsibility in what George Henry Lewes called the "perilous game" of play production; without him the fortunes of the theatre would be completely instead of only largely unpredictable.

This series of lectures will examine six theatre managers and their habits as they worked, spanning four centuries of the English-speaking stage, in an attempt to evaluate the relationship of each to the drama of his time. One of their Roman predecessors, L. Ambivius Turpio, who produced the comedies of Terence, after pointing out that he knew from experience just how uncertain were the fortunes of the stage, that the only certainty was hard work, declared his function very simply: to suit the desires of the spectators to the best of his ability *and* to make it possible for those spectators "to honor the arts of the stage."

That only five lectures, instead of the six projected, appear here is the sad but unavoidable result of Professor Downer's death in January 1970 before he was able to complete his own lecture on the American manager George Tyler (1867-1947), whose papers reflecting a lifetime of theatrical production are held in the theatre collection of the Princeton University Library. After so great a loss, those who knew him and his work have been left with the certainty that his essay on Tyler would have reinforced a deep and long-standing commitment, which he shared equally and enthusiastically with Gerald Bentley, to the theatrical profession as a significant human enterprise and to the scholarly research that recaptures, preserves, and interprets its records.

J.W.D.

Princeton, New Jersey
January 1971

Acknowledgments

Bernard Beckerman wishes to express his appreciation to Mr. A.C.L. Hall, Librarian of Dulwich College, for his kind assistance.

Barnard Hewitt is grateful to the John Simon Guggenheim Foundation for a fellowship and to the University of Illinois for a sabbatical leave which combined in 1962-63 to make possible most of the research on which the study of Stephen Price is based. For assistance in that research, he wishes particularly to thank Louis A. Rachow of the Walter Hampden Memorial Library at the Players Club, Sam Pearce of the Museum of the City of New York, Helen Willard of the Theatre Collection at Harvard University, Paul Myers of the Theatre Collection of the New York Public Library at Lincoln Center, and the staffs of the New York Historical Society, the Folger Shakespeare Library, the British Museum, and the Enthoven Collection at the Victoria and Albert Museum.

Charles Beecher Hogan makes grateful acknowledgment to the following persons in York who granted him every possible assistance: Canon R.S. Cant and Mr. C.B.L. Barr of the Minster Library; Miss Norah Gurney and Mr. Neville Webb of the Borthwick Institute of Historical Research; Mr. John Ingamells of the City Art Museum; and Mr. Maurice Smith, Librarian of the York City Library.

Contents

List of Illustrations

Pages from Philip Henslowe's diary. Reproduced from the original manuscript in The Library, Dulwich College, by permission of the Governors of Dulwich College.

Portrait of Tate Wilkinson by Stephen Hewson. Reproduced by courtesy of the City Art Gallery, York.

Playbills for performances at the Theatre Royal, York. Reproduced from the originals in the Minster Library, York, by courtesy of Canon R.S. Cant and Mr. C.B.L. Barr.

Portrait in oils of Stephen Price by Simpson, probably John Simpson (1782-1847). Reproduced by courtesy of the Walter Hampden Memorial Library in The Players.

Portion of a playbill for *Der Freischütz* as performed at the Park Theatre. Reproduced by courtesy of the New York Historical Society.

Louisa Ann Phillips as Claudia in *Rienzi* at Drury Lane Theatre. Reproduced by courtesy of the Victoria and Albert Museum, London.

John Braham, center, in the title role in *Masaniello* at Drury Lane Theatre. Reproduced by courtesy of the Enthoven Collection, Victoria and Albert Museum.

Fanny Elssler dancing "La Tarantelle." Reproduced by courtesy of the Enthoven Collection, Victoria and Albert Museum.

Portrait of Edwin Booth as Hamlet, 1870. Photograph by Napoleon Sarony, reproduced by courtesy of the Walter Hampden Memorial Library at The Players.

THE THEATRICAL MANAGER IN
ENGLAND AND AMERICA

Introduction

The Theatrical Manager and the Uses
of Theatrical Research

JOSEPH W. DONOHUE, JR.

His NAME may be as much of the moment as Harold
Prince or David Merrick, or it may be shrouded in a
reference to the "Wakefield master" or replaced by a generic term like *choregus*. If his exact identity varies, however, there is no doubt that his function is, and has always
been, the first essential for theatrical performance. Playwrights like Horace Walpole and Robert Bridges may regard with indifference or even scorn the possibilities for art
held out by production. But for the playwright whose goal
is the presentation of his work before a live audience, the
man whose attention he must first win is someone who,
though typically not an artist himself, stands in undeniable
relationship to this special and elusive art. His function is
neither to write plays nor to act in them, but to bring those
who do so together, or, stated more comprehensively, to
bring the product of their joint efforts before an audience.
It may be equally valid to say that his function is to bring
an audience to their joint product. However balanced or
phrased, the conjoining of performance and audience is his
purpose, established through centuries of theatrical history
as the prior condition for the very existence of that history
and what it chronicles. And yet, though widely recognized
for his importance, he somehow remains imperfectly under-
stood.

In the last century the director has become the object of

studies almost as extensive as those, ancient and continuing, of the actors with whom he labors. And, no matter how deep and complex his creative impulses, the dramatist and his written work need no general definition at all. But to call a man a manager, in the theatre, is to cast only an uncertain light on a figure essential to the continuing life of the form. We in fact do not even call him that any more. We use today the word *producer*, our reference being obviously to a play, whereas the word *manager* just as obviously refers, not to a play, but to the company that performs it. Producers produce plays; managers manage—theatres, one would say. But not empty theatres. They are not the overlords of mere custodial forces who ply mops and brooms in the shadows of cold auditoriums. Theirs is a full theatre, full of an audience who have come to see and hear an acting company, which the manager coordinates and which is included in the comprehensive sense of the theatre over which he presides. To call a man a manager, then, is to give him at least a historical identity, placing him in an epoch that begins somewhere around the time of the formation of cohesive professional companies in the late sixteenth and seventeenth centuries and ends sometime in the early twentieth century, perhaps with the dwindling of regional audiences, the dissolution of touring companies and the general demise of the "actor-manager" and that group identity sometimes called a "house style." At the same time, however, to use the word *manager* is to forsake the possibility of a generic term like *actor* or *director*, which makes immediate contact with well-defined areas of knowledge. We have no term, unfortunately, to comprehend the functions of *choregus*, master, manager, and producer. Where no word exists, understanding remains fragmented.

The present collection of essays on the British and American theatrical manager is an attempt to contribute to our knowledge of a subject now neglected. Scholarly fashion tends to describe any neglect as unaccountable, but in this case it is easily explained. In the first place, the ambiguity of the manager's position makes its assessment uncommonly difficult. His ultimate goal is a product we persist in thinking of as art, and his realization of it is the result of his ability to control and guide the various and often conflicting geniuses within his organization, but his work is not itself art—although it may be artful in the extreme. In the second place, the records of his endeavors are sometimes either nonexistent or else so sketchy as to be inadequate to the task of providing materials with which to build a coherent historical account. The performance of roles by actor and actress has a palpability about it that, even in imaginative retrospect, is identifiable enough. But the prior and continuing efforts of their manager to secure them as members of his company and to support their activity with a large, heterogeneous assortment of highly trained craftsmen and other skilled, or sometimes hopelessly unskilled, persons may only suggest a mad but unheroic Cuchulain fighting the waves. And that, of course, is far too romantic a metaphor for the conduct of an enterprise whose financial uncertainty can induce hysterical laughter or catatonic trance and whose activities are largely uncommittable to paper and completely irreducible to rule.

In the face of difficulty of this sort, the need to surmount it by uncovering and gathering detailed information in this single area clouded by ignorance must take precedence over the larger, and more far-reaching, task of writing a comprehensive history of production and, perhaps, of inventing an adequate generic term to identify the man who has always stood at its center. That area is, temporally speaking, the long period of something over three centuries of theatrical activity in Great Britain and America, during which the role of the manager evolved through the trial-and-error helmsmanship of Philip Henslowe at the beginning of a great mercantile age to the sophisticated navigation of Charles Wyndham in a society already veering toward a lee shore. A period that witnessed the emergence of a profound and varied dramatic literature and an equally enduring playgoing public, it has left a written legacy so rich that historians who lament the loss of what has not survived can hardly help seeming ungrateful. Yet the difficulty of writing well about the theatrical manager remains, even though his tenacious stance in the eye of the whirlwind means that many records reflect his presence. The difficulty is partly that so many of these records are fragmentary, dealing with one specialized aspect of a multifarious occupation, or are preoccupied with the contributions and interests of other people like playwrights, actors, prompters, critics, ladies of fashion, and ministers of state. The difficulty is also that, even when all available records have been searched and information combined to show how a single man effected production day after day, season after season, the chronicle seems unsatisfactory, perhaps almost lifeless. A special act of historical imagination is necessary to perceive the exertion of human personality in an age gone by. Such an act is easier to make in the case of persons like actors or playwrights or others directly associated with artistic expression, whose human qualities subserve a clear and definable function. But an imaginative act is equally necessary in the case of the theatrical manager, whose personality has been the force that holds together a thriving company (as David Garrick did) or, unhappily often, has been the means of driving audiences out of the theatre and actors to drink (as did the notorious Alfred Bunn).

The materials on which imagination concentrates are sometimes referred to, disdainfully or naively, as "raw." In this metaphor the exercise of imagination becomes a culinary art in which heat is applied and fibre broken down, the product finally being digested and assimilated. One hesitates to offer alternative metaphors. Yet it seems plain that, as an idea, the uncooked is unsatisfactory. Whatever history is composed of, it is not biodegradable. Facts are lucid entities and they can be arranged in a lucid order without disintegrating. They should not be held suspect for not being directly implicative of large generalizations. The stuff of theatrical history, like any other kind of history, is fact —information, records, data—give it what terms we like. And its painstaking unearthing and assembling are the first and obvious duty of the historian, who, no matter what his field, will sooner or later encounter the notorious laundry list or its equivalent, whose multiplication may reduce less determined minds to lint. Shakespeare can safely be above laundry lists, especially now that he is dead, but the theatrical historian had better not be.

And for this he risks being misunderstood, not because his task is any more difficult than that of the historian of military campaigns or economic depressions, but because it is related to an art form—moreover, one of a special kind whose records when assembled do not as adequately comprehend the original reality as do those put together by historians in other fields, even literary fields. An uncomfortably close analogy begins to loom here. The theatrical historian stands in much the same ambiguous relationship to the art whose history he attempts to write as does the theatrical manager to that same art, whose existence as an individual work he helps to bring into being. As much as there is need for discovering and recording exactly what it is that managers do, and at least conjecturing how they do it, there appears a need also, at this opportune time, to inquire into the nature of the process that yields understanding of this kind. The question at issue is not simply of the history that the theatrical historian writes, but of the historiography that informs it.

Seldom has the historian of the theatre stopped to explain the rationale of his calling. He has seen little need to do so. "My goal," wrote Margarete Bieber in her preface to *The History of the Greek and Roman Theatre*, "is to build out of the various elements a connected whole, a history of the theatre of the ancient world."[1] The nature and value of that whole are, the author and reader assume, self-evident.

That assumption has been with us for some time. Sheridan's Mr. Dangle in *The Critic* justifies to his wife his predilection for following the stage by quoting the committed view of an earlier, more famous amateur: "I say the stage is 'the Mirror of Nature,' and the actors are 'the Abstract, and brief Chronicles of the Time:'—and pray what can a man of sense study better?"[2] Both Hamlet and his latter-day admirer have been upheld as defenders of a general truth who have rested their case, assured of conviction.[3] Yet to skeptics like Mrs. Dangle their argument is specious, however warmly Dangle urges it to secure his place "at the head of a band of critics." Hard fact, she maintains, controverts Dangle's claim to be in touch with universals of any sort: "Ridiculous!—Both managers and authors of the least merit, laugh at your pretensions.—The Public is their Critic—without whose fair approbation they know no play can rest on the stage, and with whose applause they welcome such attacks as yours, and laugh at the malice of them, where they can't at the wit" (II, p. 195).

[1] 2nd edn. (Princeton, 1961), p. vii.

[2] *The Plays & Poems of Richard Brinsley Sheridan*, ed. R. Crompton Rhodes (Oxford, 1928), II, p. 195.

[3] See Alan S. Downer, "Mr. Dangle's Defense: Acting and Stage History," *English Institute Essays 1946* (New York, 1947), pp. 159-190.

It is not such a jaundiced view, and in any case it cannot be ignored. Sheridan—an appropriate person to make the point, since he was in his lifetime both manager and author —allows his termagant-antagonist to raise what was becoming in his day and remains in ours the dilemma of those who would study an apparently irrecoverable past. Presenting a man who with touching simplicity counts on relationships and strives for connections, Sheridan confronts him with the brutal reality of one of the riskiest of human enterprises, the theatre: Where the whim of a capricious public becomes unalterable law, what remains after the fact can be accurately recorded in the account book of a manager who may know despair at least as well as lower mathematics. And it follows that if unpredictable public response puts the intelligent contemporary critic in a limbo of his own contrivance, how much more foolish is the later observer who attempts a chronicle of things past. Records of that past remain, of course: an inscription on an ancient vase, a panoramic view of buildings along the Thames, entries in a rain-soaked and dried-out old ledger. Memorabilia, too: Kean's sword for Richard III, Sarah Siddons' make-up case. But they are merely the dregs of time. The spirit has all gone out of them. *The Rape of the Lock*, vibrant and immediate, perennially invites enjoyment, while *The Beggar's Opera* languishes in the chains of printed text and score, and revivals administer galvanic shock to the corpse of what once was original vitality. The pulse of a poem is felt in the reading of it; of a play, in the playing of it. We cannot be Pope's first audience, but we can attend to exactly what they attended to. We cannot be Gay's first audience either —nor can we hear what they heard, see what they saw. Where in one case the printing press confers immortality, in the other it serves as a mortician's aid. Managers and authors may read reviews, but meanwhile they finger receipts.

Historians of the theatre may sort scripts, identify prompt-books, examine memoirs, construct calendars, gather illustrations; they will never recapture performance. They know it. Managers know it. Everybody knows it.

This is Mrs. Dangle's rejoinder, together with some of its more disturbing implications. Although her argument may be grounded in philistinism, it serves to raise two legitimate and pressing questions that suggest the problem as a whole: Does the manager have interests or aspirations beyond his attempts to remain solvent and even to show a profit? And, regardless of aspirations, how do accounts of profit and loss, or business interests in general, relate to records of artistic performance?

We have not yet answered either question fully, for reasons that remain to be seen. The fact is that, at a certain point in its process, theatrical history becomes something different from, say, political or economic history, which can be written on the basis of surviving documents and other sorts of accumulated data, or art history, which can right-fully depend on paintings, sculptures, and other works whose preservation makes history possible. Indeed, by these standards it can be, and has been, argued that theatrical history is an invalid endeavor altogether, since the performances on which it concentrates and depends have vanished into thin air. The theatrical historian has on occasion been dismissed as no more than the incorrigible in full pursuit of the ineffable. True, as long as he remains in the area of research where the rules of evidence apply in the gathering of facts and the drawing of conclusions, the theatrical historian's discipline does not appear to differ from others. Nevertheless, there is a pair of assumptions that may underlie his work and make it, at least in its orientation, different from that of the historian of Newtonian physics or agrarian reform or evangelistic religion. These assumptions are that, although performance itself cannot be recaptured in essence, it can in some ways, or to some extent, be reconstructed and, furthermore, that sooner or later (in most cases later) the evidence and conclusions that the theatrical historian offers his reader will somehow contribute to that reconstruction, even if it consists only of an individual mental act, imaginative rather than substantive. Now, it must be emphasized that these assumptions are almost always unstated ones, and in some cases the historian may hotly deny that he holds them at all. He may take a position aligned to some extent with Mrs. Dangle's, saying that the materials he deals with are all that can be dealt with and that to go beyond them, toward some kind of imaginative, reconstructive synthesis, is mere idle speculation, not responsible scholarship. He may, in short, insist that a performance-by-performance account or a season-by-season record, amassed from five hundred obscure or commonplace sources including the ubiquitous account book and other notations of stolen delights and unpaid obligations, is a chronicle of impressive vitality in itself. That is all we know, and ever can surmise, he may contend. Meanwhile, we have the reassurance of a live theatre ongoing from that day to this and, one trusts, beyond.

To take this position it is only necessary to affirm that one's subject has an inherent appeal, an affirmation made simply by engaging in theatrical scholarship. This is, in effect, Mr. Dangle's defense. It appears, however, that an opportunity now exists to substantiate that claim more extensively. Just as we lack a full esthetic of dramatic performance, we might benefit from a more comprehensive historiography for theatrical history. It may seem temerarious to announce these needs, even more so to offer ways of answering them. Revisionism may perhaps be unwelcome, especially when a methodology has been developed and refined to the extent that even the apprentice scholar can infer from one issue of any journal in the field all he requires to support whatever project he may undertake. But it is at this point in the evolution of a discipline that it may be useful to pause, not to decide what subjects remain (there are, after all, so many) but to decide how best to understand the history that has already been written. What is proposed here is not full and systematic, as an adequate historiography should be, but is simply suggestive of certain principles that may eventually prove of value. In addition, it may help to relate the admirable factuality of much theatrical history to another, tributary study, now only in embryonic stage: the synthetic reconstruction of performance. As posited in this new approach, performance is a phenomenon that begins as the enterprise of certain persons in a particular time and place but that, as we subsequently study it, appears in a significant posture before that portion of society that composes its audience and, further, holds implicit some essential part of the culture of its age. All this, moreover, is perceived within the historical continuum that connects the production with our own day.

To make a brief test, we may consider as a hypothetical case an account of the preparation of a late eighteenth-century English play for production. The scholar's declared purpose is to present his reader with information about a familiar but nevertheless detailed and complex process. To this end he has done extensive research in the sources of the period, piecing together facts and suppositions relating to the composition of the play, the negotiations between playwright and manager, the financing, the casting of actors and actresses, the design and execution of scenery, the choosing of costumes, the copying of the actors' parts, the composition of necessary music, the setting up of machinery, the creation of special effects, the rehearsal of the play, the advertising of it in playbills and newspapers, and, finally, the performance and the response of audience and critics to it. These are simply typical aspects of the subject, undoubtedly varying from play to play and very likely augmented by explanations of particular situations and conditions or affected by gaps in the evidence.

The question begged by this account is whether it constitutes theatrical history or merely presents the "raw material," the facts, out of which theatrical history is made. There should be no hesitation about the answer. It is history. Its materials are the sources that provide the information assembled. Nor should there be any doubt that the account is supported by a coherent historiography. It may be argued, perhaps, that no account of this sort can be written without a historiography, and that in this case the rationale is the interest generated by presenting the record of a lively human enterprise in which a number of persons were involved and on whose outcome depended the continuing artistic enrichment of a sizable fraction of the city's population. Such an account, then, has an open reference to life as it was lived; its validity is experiential. In addition, its reader is clearly free to use the account for whatever purpose he likes. Seizing on the information it provides about the actual process of mounting a play on the late eighteenth-century English stage, he may wish to combine this with other similar accounts and so compile a history of theatrical production in the age. Or, considering its obvious connection with the manager's career as a public man, he may wish to integrate it with other information about his life at this time to form a chapter of a biography. Or, recognizing the importance of theatrical activity for a metropolis the size and character of London, he may use the account to help document a social history of the city. Or, impressed by its indications of concerted community effort, he may examine it anthropologically for its evidence of the bonding impulses of human beings in small groups within a larger structure. In each case, the theatrical historian has served the needs of a potentially wide readership. His accurate rendering of fact and his careful demarcation of the limits of what is known combine to generate a clear *sense of event*. The value that may be attached to it is a function of the use to which it is put. It is a value attached afterwards, in addition to its value as record.

Let us suppose, however, that the reader of the account is neither theatrical historian *per se*, nor biographer, nor social historian, nor anthropologist, but someone who wishes to relate the process of production directly to what emerges in actual performance, and who furthermore desires to build up as cogent and firm a sense of the nature and impact of this performance as the combination of evidence with interpretative imagination will allow. Such a reader must, it seems evident, begin by acknowledging the validity of the methods employed by the theatrical historian and of the historiography of event that forms their foundation. Yet it is also evident that he needs to adapt this historiography so that it may constitute a basis for the sort of study that draws on the methods, materials, and goals of various disciplines—historical, sociological, anthropological, literary—while itself not falling squarely within any one of them.

Such a historiography may be defined by describing its purpose, which is to develop a sociological esthetic of dramatic performance. The advantages of possessing a comprehensive theoretical approach to this goal would be great. We would be able to maintain a strong idea that we are dealing with art, not just with artifact; to view performance from a number of vantage points instead of being held to a single perspective; to transform what might otherwise remain picaresque excursions into an enlightened eclecticism whose limits are set by the nature of the subject and the availability of evidence, not by a prior methodology alone; and, finally, to remain aware that we do all this from a point in time that is itself moving forward. Our sense of dramatic performance as *motion* and of our correlative movement as we view it must be a precedent for whatever we discover. To wish to be at the still point of a turning world may reveal a natural longing for permanence, but to think either of past dramatic performance or of our own present study of it in this way is naive. No theoretical approach to performance will be adequate if it ignores the evanescent nature of the art. The revels have already ended before we even begin. To suggest that we can achieve a re-creation is only fantasy—but to maintain that all that can be known lies in the surviving records of an insubstantial pageant is, I think, to impoverish needlessly the possibilities of our study. I believe we may legitimately try to find a way of apprehending the virtual character of a real process while, at the same time, ranging out from it in various directions to recapture as much as possible the conditions that governed both performance and reception. To do so will be to develop, out of the historiography of event, a historiography of enactment.

In this approach—presently still tentative and unproved—we may begin by recognizing that the kind of awareness, and the kinds of assumptions, that we ourselves take with us when we go to the theatre are analogous to those possessed by audiences of other decades and ages. Study of performed plays leads to discovering and describing a number of related dimensions, esthetic and otherwise, including the dimension, difficult but so important to define, of the modern audience's and reader's involvement in the art of the past. Bearing in mind the partly analogical nature of our understanding, while at the same time striving to avoid mere solipsistic response, we may proceed to examine the dimensions of the subject in question. It is important here to remember that the point of contact between performance and audience is the focal point of our study. As we do so, complementary ways of understanding the drama of the day begin to clarify themselves: Performance appears as varied theatrical entertainment and spirited commercial endeavor; as a craft in which experience falls within familiar conventions or is shaped into new, experimental forms; as unwitting expression of deep beliefs and broadly held assumptions, desires, and fears; and as a conscious social act habitually performed by both players and playgoers.

In 1965 Jean Duvignaud published his study entitled *L'Acteur: Esquisse d'une sociologie du comédien* (Paris, Gallimard). Duvignaud points out that there are, or have been, two words to describe the person who embodies character on the stage: *acteur, comédien*. We would say *actor, player*. The essence of the distinction is that in the first instance one is speaking of the performer in relation to his art, whereas the latter term refers to the performer in relation to his audience. Duvignaud's essay requires that, for a comprehensive understanding of what happens in performance, we must take both meanings as applicable.[4] Performance while in progress is the test of actor, playwright, and other professionals concerned, but it is as well, by implication, a measure of the identity of the audience. Afterwards, it is the focal point for reconstruction. In order to "see" it properly, we must, paradoxically, be aware of what lies in the shadows offstage or, even more obscured, in the mentalities and social backgrounds and cultural assumptions of both

---

[4] Duvignaud's more extended study, *Sociologie du Théâtre: Essai sur les ombres collectives* (Paris, P.U.F., 1965), is of great importance despite the apparent lack of recognition it has, together with his book on actors, so far received.

actor-player and audience. In short, we may employ a historiography of enactment to arrive at a sociological esthetic of dramatic performance.

This is not to say, however, that a newly developed historiography will supersede the one already established. The student of enactment will in practical ways continue to rely on the historians of event, not only because their methods are adaptable to his special interest but because historians produce a large share of the factual accounts that, in turn, may contribute to the virtual synthesis of reconstructed performance, just as they already do to social and cultural history, to biography, and to other disciplinary and interdisciplinary interests. In any case, if the historiography of enactment proves to afford a valuable approach to theatrical studies, it will not meet the objections of Mrs. Dangle any more than the historiography of event now does. No argument can prevail against a resolute defender of the balance sheet as sole guide to conduct and measure of success.

Yet it is true that theatrical managers themselves have been known to hold this view, and even to stake hard-won reputations on it. It is true also that the theatre—responsive, more than any other traditional form, to the public voice—depends for continuity, for life itself, on the rapport a successful manager and his company achieve with that highly vocal public. This is why study of the theatrical manager is so crucial a necessity for the historian. But such study is necessary for others too. It is only the theatre that, perhaps expectedly, produces a Kyd or a Davenant, a Shirley or a Cibber, that on occasion has the great good fortune to discover a Shakespeare or a Congreve. To slight either the genius of the great dramatist or the talents of his more workaday contemporaries is to distort and falsify what might otherwise become a full account of the nature of dramatic art and the nature of its performance before an audience. At the center of that activity, as the following essays demonstrate, the theatrical manager is to be found. Examination of his function must begin with the presentation of a record as rich in continuity as sources permit. Then and only then can generalization take place. And if reconstruction of some kind takes place as well, it will do so not on the basis of an impressionistic reading of the text of the play, but by virtue of clearly established records of events, whose accumulation must remain a prior necessity for an adequate understanding of the experience they frame.

Philip Henslowe

BERNARD BECKERMAN

O N THE FIRST sheet of the account book known as his *Diary*, Philip Henslowe scribbled the wry observation, "when I lent I wasse A friend & when I asked I wasse unkind."[1] This plaintive comment epigrammatizes the twofold activity of Henslowe's business life. It is an acknowledgment of the fickle ambivalence of his financial dealings, an ambivalence that characterizes Henslowe's entire career. That his life alternated between dispensing and collecting

---

[1] The principal sources for any study of Philip Henslowe are the manuscripts and documents bequeathed to the College of God's Gift at Dulwich by its founder, Edward Alleyn. Although the entire collection has never been reproduced, significant portions of it, especially those dealing with Henslowe's and Alleyn's theatrical affairs, have been printed several times. Henslowe's account book, the so-called *Diary*, was edited by W. W. Greg in 1904. This edition superseded the earlier abstract of the *Diary* printed by Edmund Malone (1790) and reprinted by James Boswell the younger (1821), as well as the fuller version issued by J. P. Collier (1845). R. A. Foakes and R. T. Rickert supplied a new edition of the *Diary* in 1961. Greg also edited a selection of supplementary documents as *Henslowe Papers*. To facilitate reference to either the Greg or the Foakes and Rickert edition of the *Diary*, citation in the text is made by folio page (viz., f.9). Greg follows the pagination of the *Diary*, so that in his edition the folio page number may be found in the upper right corner of the *recto* page. Foakes and Rickert do not follow the original pagination; instead, they print the folio page number in bold face and encase it in brackets on the left of each page. The following abbreviations are utilized in the notes:

Greg, *Diary*	*Henslowe's Diary*, ed. W. W. Greg (London, 1904-08), Vol. I, *The Diary*; Vol. II, *Commentary*.
Papers	*Henslowe Papers*, ed. W. W. Greg (London, 1907).
Foakes & Rickert	*Henslowe's Diary*, ed. R. A. Foakes and R. T. Rickert (Cambridge, 1961).

money in connection with a wide variety of theatrical and nontheatrical enterprises is clear enough. Less clear, particularly in respect to his theatrical activities, is exactly how he conducted his affairs and what role he played in the theatrical life of Shakespeare's day.

There is no question that Henslowe was a theatrical landlord. It is equally clear that he performed some sort of banking function for a number of theatrical companies. Beyond that, his part is shadowy. He has been called "a shrewd theatrical investor," "a famous Elizabethan theatre-manager," and "a general banker and business manager."[2] W. W. Greg, in his definitive edition of the *Diary*, refers to Henslowe variously as a banker, entrepreneur, and impresario. E. K. Chambers is more conservative. To him Henslowe was simply a landlord and financier.[3] Recent writers such as Glynne Wickham and C. Walter Hodges have credited Henslowe with an important voice in the shaping of theatrical history. Wickham speaks of him as a key figure in "a growing tendency towards monopoly in theatrical management which after 1660 became total."[4] Hodges calls Henslowe "the most enterprising manager of theatrical affairs of his day."[5] On the face of it, the different terms applied to Henslowe do not seem mutually exclusive. Each designates one part or another of the total responsibility undertaken by a theatrical manager or producer. Yet the very diversity of terms used by theatre historians betrays

[2] Alois Nagler, *Shakespeare's Stage* (New Haven, 1958), p. 12; Harold Jenkins, *The Life and Work of Henry Chettle* (London, 1934), p. 19; R. B. Sharpe, *The Real War of the Theatres* (Boston, 1935), p. 5.

[3] Greg, *Diary*, II, pp. 120, 130; E. K. Chambers, *The Elizabethan Stage* (Oxford, 1923), II, p. 139.

[4] Glynne Wickham, *Early English Stages* (New York, 1963), II, p. 134.

[5] C. Walter Hodges, *The Globe Restored*, 2nd ed. (London, 1968), p. 116.

an underlying uncertainty about the work Henslowe did.[6] "Landlord," "banker," "manager"—all denote quite different degrees of involvement in and responsibility for theatrical production. If, for example, one calls Henslowe a theatrical manager, does one mean thereby that Henslowe made the significant decisions respecting engagement of actors, choice of repertory, and exploitation of production?

The three terms Greg applies to Henslowe may very well encompass the principal activities of the theatrical manager or producer as he functions today. He must be banker, impresario, and entrepreneur, or at least fulfill the tasks proper to each position. The manager or producer is banker, not necessarily in the sense of funding theatrical productions himself, but of securing the funds either by having access to credit or by attracting investment. That part of him that is impresario sells the theatrical product he has funded. He excites public attention in order to advertise his product. Last, in his role of entrepreneur, he acts as a catalyst. He may transport a successful performance from one city to another, he may bring actors and writers together in a new combination, he may encourage ability and nurse it to fruition. It is this entrepreneurial side that is most reminiscent of traditional theatre management. In former days, the manager or-

---

6 In his exposition of Chettle's relations with Henslowe, Harold Jenkins exemplifies the uncertainty that I mention. As I noted earlier, Jenkins refers to Henslowe as a "theatre-manager" (p. 19) though observing that he "did not buy plays; but [merely] financed the [Admiral's] Company, lending them the money they required to obtain plays" (pp. 21-22). Nevertheless, Jenkins refers to Henslowe's "right to [a] play" (p. 21) and attributes a mercenary quality to Henslowe (pp. 20-21) whereby he deliberately kept "the poverty-stricken dramatists in debt to him" (p. 22). Thus, within the space of a few pages, two contradictory views emerge: on one hand, Henslowe was an "astute and business-like" (p. 20) force in theatrical affairs; on the other, he was a passive financier for the Admiral's and Worcester's companies.

ganized his own company and produced his own plays. As entrepreneur, the contemporary producer joins talents temporarily in order to create a specific product. Without necessarily producing anything himself, he sparks production in others.

Neither "manager" nor "producer" was a theatrical term in Henslowe's day. Shakespeare does indeed have Theseus call for his "manager of mirth" in *A Midsummer Night's Dream* (V.i.35), but this phrase is used in a descriptive rather than a professional sense. Among the players of that time, there was no word to designate the person who administered business affairs for a theatre, principally because the theatre had been a cooperative venture for so long. Not until the middle of the eighteenth century was "manager" widely used in theatrical parlance,[7] and "producer" became current even later.

At the heart of sixteenth-century commercial production was the acting company. It was the company that held the patent granting the members the right to perform and protecting them, in some measure at least, from civic or clerical interference. It was the company that initiated the production process. It was the company that provided virtually the only free market for a writer's wares. To understand the possible scope of Henslowe's activities in theatrical affairs, we need to review, even if briefly, the nature of the acting company as it affected management.

Organizationally, the company was a partnership of master actors, bound together by common agreement and patent authority. Consisting of nine to twelve sharers, this partnership as an entity undertook management responsibility. It hired actors, commissioned dramatists, engaged craftsmen, and rented playhouses. During most of the six-

[7] The earliest usage of "manager" in connection with theatrical business is dated in 1764 by the Oxford English Dictionary.

teenth century it retained its cooperative character, management chores being widely distributed among the sharers. Increasingly, however, a company's business activities grew more complex. With the erection of permanent playhouses, beginning in 1576, a company either had to raise money for its own building or come to terms with someone who could provide it. With permanence came the pressure for more ambitious production and thus for the accumulation of costumes and properties, calling for still further capitalization. Simultaneously, the Crown centralized the theatre by restricting the number of allowed troupes as well as the permissible number of patrons: to barons of the realm and higher in 1572 and to members of the royal family in 1604. These changes meant that only the well-organized and properly financed companies could hope to survive, requiring as a result more specialized management than had been customary. Such a development may be reflected in the history of the Accounts of the Treasurer's Chamber. Until 1594, over 80 percent of Court payments to players designate the company as payee. From 1594 onward every payment designates one or more actors by name,[8] suggesting that a degree of specialization set in after this date, or rather tended to set in, for a clear differentiation of function did not occur immediately. Thus, when Philip Henslowe became involved in theatrical affairs at the end of the sixteenth century, he encountered a strong tradition of group management on one hand, and a changing theatrical economy on the other.

Although the date of Philip Henslowe's birth is unknown, his life was roughly contemporary and almost exactly coterminous with Shakespeare's. Both men died in the first

[8] *Dramatic Records in the Declared Accounts of the Treasurer of the Chamber* 1558-1642. The Malone Society Collection. VI (1961-62), *passim.*

quarter of 1616. From testimony of his son-in-law, the actor Edward Alleyn, we learn that Henslowe married a widow, Agnes Woodward, about 1580. Before his marriage, Henslowe was, according to Alleyn, a servant to the widow, and "shee having a likinge or affection [for him] did . . . marrie and take him to husband."[9] She was older than he, by many years it was said. Fortunately for Henslowe, she was well-to-do, perhaps even wealthy, and apparently provided him with the capital for his investments. These begin in the mid-fifteen-eighties. On 14 June 1584 he and Richard Nicolson, a leather dresser, formed a partnership to convert goatskins into Spanish leather.[10] This investment indicates that Henslowe may indeed have been "a dyer," as he is called in the agreement.

Less than a year later, Henslowe embarked upon the acquisition of real estate, an activity in which he engaged, though somewhat fitfully, throughout his lifetime. On 24 March 1585 he took a lease on the Little Rose estate, a parcel of land lying on the southern side of the Thames in an area known as the Bankside. For what purpose he initially made the purchase we do not know, but by 1587 he had decided to erect a playhouse on the property, and during 1587-88 he completed construction of the Rose theatre. This was the first of his many theatrical enterprises, all of which I shall consider in detail later. His non-theatrical dealings continued to involve real estate and branched into money-lending. He seems to have been active in both kinds of businesses in 1586. From 16 January 1593 to at least April 1596 he was engaged in or underwriting a pawnbroking

[9] Testimony of Edward Alleyn, 21 July 1617 in Star Chamber Proceedings cited by Charles Sisson, "Henslowe's Will Again," *Review of English Studies,* v (1929), p. 310.

[10] Muniments 86-87 cited by Remington P. Patterson, *Philip Henslowe and the Rose Theatre* (Unpublished doctoral dissertation, Yale, 1957), p. 8.

business. After 1595 he began to acquire more substantial real estate holdings, mainly on the Bankside, buying tenements, at least one inn, and probably brothels or at least buildings in which the brothels were housed. By 1596 he had defined the scope of his activities, thereafter deepening and expanding them, but not shifting to other enterprises. Thus, besides his theatrical concerns, his investments in land and tenements occupied his attention for the rest of his life.

Henslowe's first theatrical investment, as we have seen, was the Rose playhouse. Apparently, he undertook the erection of this building alone, but in the course of its construction entered into partnership with one of the tenants of his Little Rose property, a grocer named John Cholmley. Their deed of 10 January 1587 is written to cover a period of eight years and three months.[11] Since Henslowe was to pay the full cost of construction and repairs until 29 September, it is reasonable to assume, first, that he had sufficient funds in reserve, and second, that the anticipated date for completion of construction was about 1 October 1587. Thereafter, the two partners were to share costs and income, and in addition, toward his share in the investment, Cholmley was to contribute £816, or £25.10s. per quarter. The purpose of this arrangement is puzzling. Greg presumes that Henslowe entered into the partnership either because he lacked adequate financing himself or because he wished to spread the risk.[12] It is more likely that if Henslowe agreed to repayment over an eight-year period, he had money in hand for construction. Henslowe was entering into a new business enterprise. Unlike John Brayne, another grocer, who had entered into partnership with the theatrically experienced

---

[11] Muniment no. 16. A major portion of the deed is reprinted in Foakes and Rickert, pp. 304-306, as well as in *Papers*, pp. 2-4.
[12] Greg, *Diary*, II, p. 44.

James Burbage in the construction of the Theatre (1576), Henslowe had no knowledgeable person upon whom he could rely. Therefore, in all likelihood, he attempted to minimize the risk attendant on operating the playhouse. Unfortunately, we do not know if the deed of partnership between Cholmley and him was ever executed. When Henslowe began to record expenses and income for the playhouse in 1591-92, he made no relevant mention of Cholmley, a lack that suggests that the partnership never went into operation or that it was dissolved before the expiration of the eight-year, three-month term.

However that arrangement turned out, the Rose was in fact completed, probably by the end of October 1587, when it seems to be mentioned in a Privy Council order of the 29th, and certainly by April 1588, when the Sewer Records describe it as "new."[13] How it was occupied until 1591 is open to conjecture. That it had a steady occupant is unlikely. The years 1588 to 1594 were years of change in the composition and organization of many companies, a change accelerated by the severe plague that broke out in 1592. Not until June 1594 was stability restored to theatrical activity. Thus, in the first six years of his involvement in theatrical business, Henslowe must have undergone an unprofitable and chaotic experience. For example, between February of 1592 and mid-1594, four different companies played at the Rose, but their cumulative occupancy amounted to no more than seven months, or less than one day in four. Yet despite this hardship, these years had one far-reaching result. Not only did Henslowe come to know the theatrical fraternity as a whole, but he also met and established close personal and business connections with Edward Alleyn.

The importance of the Alleyn alliance to Henslowe's for-

[13] Joseph Quincy Adams, *Shakespearean Playhouses* (Boston, 1917), p. 145.

tunes cannot be overestimated. Late in life, Philip admitted "that he was much beholden unto . . . Allin. And that . . . [he] could never have effected those things which hee did, but by the help and care of the said Allin."[14] That Edward Alleyn was an enterprising and vigorous personality there is no doubt. By the time he was sixteen years old, he owned a share in Worcester's men. Later he joined the Admiral's men and henceforth retained his title as one of the Lord Admiral's servants, regardless of the company with which he played. Recognized as one of the most skillful and commanding actors of the age, he also possessed marked business ability. As early as 1589, he and his brother John purchased theatrical stock and clothing, ostensibly for resale. At the age of twenty-six, he married Henslowe's step-daughter Joan.

Thereafter, we find traces of Alleyn's accounts intermixed with Henslowe's. Henslowe seems to have been keeping track of and possibly supervising expenses in connection with Alleyn's new house, and occasionally he recorded other purchases. Whether or not he was actually serving as his son-in-law's agent in these matters, he was closely involved in Alleyn's business affairs. How involved is difficult to say. Alleyn's affairs must have been much more extensive than Henslowe's accounts indicate, for these do not record the source of Alleyn's mounting prosperity. In 1594 Alleyn bought the Bear Garden for £450,[15] and in 1596 he had sufficient wealth to commit himself to a lease of £3000 (f.24). From these scraps of information, a consistent image of Alleyn emerges: independent, shrewd, socially ambitious, and, according to his letters, amiable though condescend-

14 Testimony of Joan Horton in *Henslow* v. *Henslow* as quoted by William Rendle, "Philip Henslowe," *Genealogist*, n.s. IV (1887), p. 154.
15 Account in Edward Alleyn's memorandum book, printed by Foakes and Rickert, p. 301.

ing. He is ever present in Henslowe's life, and our understanding of Henslowe's contribution to the theatre must
always reckon with Alleyn's presence.

For convenience, Henslowe's known theatrical activities
can be divided into four periods. The first extends from
early 1592 to 1596-97. It is his Rose period. The second
spans the years from 1597-98 to early 1604. It is the late
Rose and early Fortune playhouse period. From 1604 to
1611 Henslowe was deeply involved in the game of bears,
bulls, and mastiff dogs, commonly known as baiting. This
may be termed his Bear Garden period. Last, from 1611 to
his death in 1616, he combined his theatrical and baiting
activities in a new playhouse, the Hope, so we might speak
of the Hope period. Each of the periods not only distin-
guishes a different playhouse in which Henslowe concen-
trated his efforts, but also marks changing relationships
between Henslowe and his theatrical associates.

The position of theatrical landlord was a precarious one
during the first part of the Rose period. Early in 1592 Henslowe laid out £121 for repairs on the Rose. Considering
that the building of a new playhouse would cost about
£500, it is evident that Henslowe either had to make major
repairs or was determined to make major improvements.
Shortly after the work was completed or perhaps even
while it was under way, Lord Strange's men began an
extended engagement at the Rose on 19 February 1592
(f.7). Greg believes that Alleyn may have then been connected with Strange's men, as he had been before this time
and was to become later.[16] If so, the appearance of Strange's
men at the Rose may have occurred through Alleyn's influence, and Henslowe's substantial outlay might reflect the
growing association of the two men.

[16] W. W. Greg, "Edward Alleyn," in *Shakespeare and the Theatre*.
Papers of the Shakespeare Association 1925-26 (London, 1927), p. 5.

Unfortunately, circumstances defeated, for a time at least, this new beginning. On 23 June, the Privy Council issued an order prohibiting all performances until Michaelmas, and Henslowe recorded the last performance of this engagement on 22 June (f.8). Playing could not resume in September, however, for a serious outbreak of the plague occurred during the summer, and the prohibition was continued. On 22 October Alleyn married Henslowe's stepdaughter and seems to have joined the Henslowe household while his own house was being prepared. On 29 December 1592 Strange's men made another attempt to resume playing at the Rose, but were able to continue only until the end of January before the virulence of the plague put an end to playing in London for the rest of the year. It may be relevant that Henslowe began his pawnbroking business in the middle of January 1593. His playhouse had lain empty for six months, and, although occupied at the moment, could not be assured a tenant in those disturbed times. Conducting the business through his nephew Francis, Henslowe may have conceived of pawnbroking as a temporary expedient. By April 1596 he seems to have discontinued it.

The first half of 1594 witnessed a series of abortive starts at the Rose. First, Sussex's men played there for about six weeks (27 December 1593 to 6 February 1594) (f.8ᵛ), then sometime later Sussex's joined with the Queen's men to play for one week (1-8 April), and a month later the Admiral's men played for three days (14-16 May). Several weeks later, there occurred a curious engagement that has not been fully explicated. From 3 June to 13 June (f.9) the Admiral's men and the Chamberlain's men combined forces and played together, not at the Rose, but at a playhouse located some distance from the Bankside at Newington Butts. By

15 June the Admiral's men were back at the Rose alone,[17] and entered upon a period of fairly continuous perform-ance until mid-1597.

The interpretation of these events is a tricky matter. Throughout the summer of 1593 Alleyn was touring with Strange's men. Sometime between then and May 1594 Alleyn, together with former members of the old Worces-ter's company as well as newer members from Strange's, reconstituted the Admiral's company. In this task it is likely that Alleyn took the lead, and it is even more likely that his close association with Henslowe was instrumental in bring-ing the newly formed troupe to the Rose. But why did the Admiral's men play for only three days in May before laying over three weeks, and then combine with the Chamberlain's men at Newington Butts? Greg conjectures that a need for repairs led to interruption of playing at the Rose in May, and Chambers supposes that the increase of the plague may have led to a further restraint of playing.[18] I should like to supply a third explanation.

Throughout the spring there had been a sequence of interrupted engagements, each engagement terminating after increasingly shorter runs. That the Chamberlain's men were forced to join the Admiral's men at Newington Butts makes it evident that this alliance was caused not only by circumstances at the Rose, but by playing conditions in general. Whatever interrupted the earlier engagement of the Sussex-Queen's men seems to have precipitately dis-rupted the schedule of the Admiral's men too. It may have been a renewal of the plague. Or the danger of the plague

---

[17] Greg, *Diary*, II, pp. 84-85. Although the change to the Rose is not specified by Henslowe, Greg's interpretation of the continuous entries in the *Diary* (f.9) is generally accepted.

[18] Greg, *Diary*, II, p. 84; Chambers, II, p. 140.

may have been used as a lever by the authorities to keep the playhouses closed. After all, prior to the epidemic the Privy Council had ordered the closing of all theatres for political reasons. My conjecture is that the union of the Admiral's and the Chamberlain's men at Newington Butts was a compromise agreed upon by the Council, perhaps with the intention that it be made a permanent arrangement. If so, we can well imagine the pressure exerted by Alleyn, the Burbages, and Henslowe, if at that time he had any influence, to dissolve this partnership. Within ten days they were successful, and each company returned to its own playhouse.

If this interpretation is correct, why then was Henslowe involved with the Newington Butts playhouse at all, and why did he record income from it? Obviously, he had a vital stake in limiting the Newington Butts engagement to as brief a period as possible. His later profits from the Rose make that clear. Probably through Alleyn, he had come to an agreement with the Admiral's men to provide them with a playhouse. To fulfill this agreement, he may have had to rent Newington Butts temporarily. It has been taken for granted that in doing so Henslowe was acting for the Chamberlain's men as well as the Admiral's men. But we must allow for another explanation. If the Admiral's and the Chamberlain's men had a joint arrangement, it may very well have extended to the rental of the playhouse. In that case, Henslowe would have continued to represent the Lord Admiral's men alone, and his takings would reflect his share from only *half* the earnings at Newington Butts. Greg explains the sudden increase of income after 15 June as the result of the return to the Bankside by the Admiral's men. But if a contributory reason was that the later receipts reflected a share from the *full* earnings of the Rose, it would not only better explain why the earnings jumped nearly five-fold[19] but also indicate that Henslowe had a more limited role in this engagement than has been hitherto supposed. After 15 June, Henslowe's arrangement with the Admiral's men became normalized for the duration of the Rose period.

What was that arrangement? Throughout the early Rose period, Henslowe dealt with the Admiral's men solely as a landlord. His connection with Alleyn may have assured steady occupancy of the playhouse, but did not mean that Henslowe was involved in the internal affairs of the company. For providing the house and keeping it in repair he received half the admission fees to the galleries, an arrangement common in the public playhouses. His *Diary* preserves a daily record of the plays performed by the actors and the monies earned by Henslowe during the entire period. Since this record constitutes the bulk of his theatrical accounts in these years, we can assume that his dealings with the company were limited. At the same time he was amassing non-theatrical real estate, from which fact we can conclude that Henslowe was principally active as a landowner and landlord.

One type of nontheatrical account is of interest at this point. Since Henslowe disbursed a wide variety of business and non-business loans in later years, it might be illuminating to see how the practice started. In 1594 he began to make fairly frequent loans to individuals: first to friends, relatives, and business associates; later to a few select players. Only after 1596 did loans become more widespread. These early loans seem to have been purely personal, and the fact that they were first made to Hens-

---

[19] The earnings between 3 June and 13 June averaged slightly more than 9s. a day; those between 15 June and 26 June averaged slightly more than 43s. per day (f.9).

lowe's intimates argues that they were not primarily profit-making, if indeed profit was a factor at all. In examining the more extensive loans later on, it is well to remember the genesis of these personal loans.

The second period, spanning the late Rose and early Fortune years, has no distinct beginning. It emerges from an upsetting and turbulent transition. Between mid-1596 and 1598, the Admiral's men faced a series of crises that combined to disturb the relative stability of the Rose period and bring the company to the edge of disaster. As a result of these troubled months, Henslowe became more deeply embroiled in the daily affairs of the players.

Fortunately, the improvised character of Henslowe's accounting practice enables us to follow the history of this transition with fair accuracy. Because entries are scattered through the *Diary*, and the bookkeeping does not follow a chronological sequence, it is possible at times to identify the stages of Henslowe's changing relationship with the actors. This is particularly true during the years 1596-98. To trace the changes, however, does require minute examination of the evidence.

A harbinger of change appears in May 1596. For the first time, the Admiral's men borrowed money from Henslowe. This they did through Edward Alleyn, who served both as payee and payor for the company. Between 6 May and 25 May he borrowed £21.13s.4d. Later he borrowed additional sums, bringing the total amount borrowed to £39.10s. (f.71ᵛ). Entered beneath these loans is an itemized list of repayments made by Alleyn between 10 May and 8 July, amounting to £39.9s.[20] Apparently, Henslowe

[20] The reason for the difference between the loan of £39.10s. and the repayment of £39.9s. is not clear. A further confusion arises from the insertion of the figure £33.0s.4d. at the top of the page above a record for £21.13s.4d. This figure cannot be reconciled with any other

extended a short-term loan to the company which was paid off expeditiously. Here again, we see that the transaction had a personal rather than a business basis.

The loan is but one symptom that the Admiral's men were undergoing severe strain. Remington Patterson points out that during the course of 1596 Henslowe's daily income dropped to its lowest since 1592.[21] In 1596 the average yield was 28s. compared to a range of 30s.9d. to 35s.9d. in the previous years, the daily average from 1592 to 1595 being 34s.6d. This drop of income, paralleling as it must a similar drop in company income, explains the series of loans in May.

By October the company was once again borrowing from Henslowe, once again with the expectation of short-term financing. Although the entries for these loans are somewhat difficult to follow, their very complication enables us to reconstruct the shifting relations between Henslowe and the actors.[22] Beginning 14 October, Henslowe entered loans against the company, specifying Edward Alleyn, Martin Slater, James Donstall, and Edward Juby as responsible agents. He begins the account on a partly filled page (f.23/II:11). Apparently not expecting to make many loans to the company, Henslowe did not leave much room for subsequent entries. Instead, he drew a line above the

---

figures on the page although it comes closest to an interim total of £32.3s.4d. borrowed by Alleyn (f.71v). The figure of £33.0s.4d. represents either a previous debt, which I doubt, since there is no record of earlier outlays to the company, or an erroneous interim accounting.

21 Patterson, p. 201.

22 To appreciate fully the improvisatory and unsystematic entries in Henslowe's accounts at this time, one must examine the original document. Therefore, I have reproduced facsimiles of the relevant pages together with a descriptive key. See Plates I and II for f.22v and f.23. In the text Roman numerals designate plates, succeeding arabic numerals designate a line in the accounts.

lower third of the page and, on 29 October, began entering repayments (II:26). But after the second payment on All Hallows Day (1 November), and before the third payment on 13 December, Henslowe extended further loans to the players. Not having space on the initial page, he began a new set of debits on the opposite sheet (f.22^v/I:13). Although extending from the end of November to 14 March, they cover advances mainly for the first half of December. There was no borrowing in January and February, and, except for a very small undated payment to a carter, Henslowe recorded no loan to the company between 16 December and 7 March 1597.

On both pages Henslowe kept a running balance of advances and repayments. These periodic balances are inserted between lines and in margins, illustrating the improvised character of these dealings (II:26-31). They also show how quickly expenditures outran returns, to such an extent that during January the company vigorously exerted itself to clear its accounts. Its four repayments between 29 October and 4 January come to £6. Its three repayments for the rest of January come to £16 (f.23/II:32-36). Since payments of these larger sums coincided with higher receipts for new plays (f.25^v), it seems evident that the company was engaged in a crash program to rid itself of debt. It does not seem to have been successful, however, for on 24 January Henslowe began a new form of recording his receipts. Divided into five columns, it lists income in two of these columns. The purpose of the other three columns has not yet been satisfactorily fathomed, and the matter is too complicated to deal with here.[23] What does seem reasonable, however, is that the new accounts embodied a method for systematically recording extended repayments

[23] Foakes and Rickert, pp. xxxiii-xxxvi, summarize the principal theories concerning these columns and offer a new one of their own.

of small sums. Taken altogether, then, the early entries followed by the five-columnar plan reveal the *ad hoc* growth of Henslowe's arrangements, and certainly indicate that, at first, Henslowe regarded them as temporary.

The difficulties of the Admiral's men are further reflected in the fact that they gave no plays at Court in 1596-97. A year earlier they had given four performances, and their failure to appear at Court after a poor year may be read either as a symptom of cumulative difficulties throughout 1596 or as a prefiguring of further difficulties to come. For the difficulties did indeed continue. Sometime in the spring of 1597, at least two and possibly five of the sharers in the Admiral's men left the Rose and went to the Swan, where they performed with others as Pembroke's men.[24] The occasion for this defection is not clear, nor is there certainty as to who initiated it. At a later date the actors charged that the move was brought about through the persuasiveness of the Swan's owner, Francis Langley. Langley, on the other hand, claimed that the actors "have been earnest suiters . . . to have [his] howse for to playe in."[25] Whoever the instigator, the actors seemed willing enough to try their luck in the recently built Swan.

Their luck was not good, as it turned out. The new company, through either miscalculation or audacity, seems

[24] C. W. Wallace, "The Swan Theatre and the Earl of Pembroke's Servants," *Englische Studien*, XLIII (1910-11), pp. 357-358, asserts that Robert Shaw, Richard Jones, Thomas Downton, Gilbert Spenser, and William Borne (alias Bird) left the Lord Admiral's men for Pembroke's, their defection forcing the former company to suspend playing between 13 February and 3 March 1597. Patterson, p. 200, follows him and offers the same reason for the interruption in the Admiral's schedule. Chambers, however, lists only two Admiral's men who joined the Earl of Pembroke's men at the Swan, namely Richard Jones and Thomas Downton (*Elizabethan Stage*, II, pp. 150-151). He is probably correct, for Shaw and Borne's names do not appear in the *Diary* before August 1597 and Spenser's before October 1597.

[25] Wallace, p. 359.

to have offended the authorities in July 1597 by presenting
The Isle of Dogs. The Privy Council immediately closed all
theatres and prohibited all plays until 1 November. This
closure destroyed the Pembroke-Langley alliance and
finally led to the amalgamation of Pembroke's with the
Admiral's men. It is at this point that we at last see
Henslowe taking an active role in company operation.
Throughout the summer he strove to bring the Admiral
defectors back to the Rose and to attract other members of
the Pembroke company. Unlike Langley, he was able to
obtain a license to reopen his playhouse, and thus could
offer the best chance for employment. He seems also to
have adopted at least one of Langley's methods. He
required two of the defectors as well as two former
Pembroke men to post bond with him, guaranteeing that
they would play nowhere else but at the Rose for the next
three years.[26] These bonds are curious instruments. They

[26] In *Shaw et al. v. Langley*, it is clear that Langley required the
players to sign a bond of £100 each before they commenced playing
at the Swan 21 February 1597 (Wallace, pp. 345-346, 349). There is
no evidence that Henslowe required actors to bind themselves to the
Rose before this date. The particular entries in the *Diary* (ff.230v,
231, 232, 232v, 233), as Chambers noted (II, p. 154), may or may not
indicate that formal articles were drawn. In examining these entries,
we must make a distinction between hiring and bonding. Between
27 July 1597 and 18 November 1598 we find eleven entries concerning
twelve men. Four or possibly five (the entry for William Borne, f.232,
states Borne "came & ofered hime sealfe to come and playe wth my
lord admeralles mean") indicate that the actors bound themselves to
play at the Rose. These are dated between 3 August and 6 October
1597. Except for the first entry for John Helle, the duration of the
bond is three years. Chambers minimizes the distinction between these
bonds and other forms of hiring (II, p. 154). Yet in the evolution of
Henslowe's role in the theatre, the four bonds taken of Richard Jones
(6 August), Robert Shaw (6 August), William Borne (10 August),
and Thomas Downton (6 October) are peculiarly significant. Jones
and Downton had left the Lord Admiral's men for Pembroke's in
February; Shaw and Borne had been Pembroke's men before the

did not make the actors employees of the playhouse owner, for the company remained the production unit. Nevertheless, the inauguration of bonded players was an incursion of the landlord into the internal affairs of the company, and, as such, a herald of the future.

Why did Henslowe require bonds at this date? Langley's competition was certainly sufficient cause to drive Henslowe to this expedient. But a far more vital reason, I believe, led to his increased participation in company matters. Hitherto, Henslowe's link to the Admiral's men had been through Edward Alleyn. The company was committed to the Rose more through Alleyn's influence than through any legal obligation. Yet even his influence had not prevented players from leaving the Rose for the Swan. Worst of all, between the closing of the playhouses on 28 July and the reopening of the Rose on 11 October, Alleyn decided to retire from the stage.[27] He continued to witness agreements and perhaps advise Henslowe, but he no longer was the inside man in the Henslowe-Alleyn partnership. Consequently, Henslowe was driven to establish a new understanding with the players. This was not easy. By tradition and organization, the acting company was a closed body of equal sharers. The landlord could insist on bonds

---

playhouses were closed. The bonds were sealed before playing resumed on 11 October. Thus, they seem to be instruments for guaranteeing that these former Pembroke men would not disrupt the Lord Admiral's men on joining the company.

[27] The exact date of Alleyn's retirement is not known. He does not appear in Henslowe's list of Admiral's men responsible for loans after 11 October 1597 (f.43ᵛ), although he does serve as witness for loans as late as 8 December. Henslowe also notes purchases "sence my sonne edward allen leafte [p]laynge," the first item being dated 29 December. Since as Henslowe's son-in-law and friend Alleyn could have still served as a witness after leaving the company, I think it more likely that he retired before the resumption of playing at the Rose.

from individual actors, but if they left him his only recourse was to legal retaliation. As a bulwark against loss, the bonds had some use; as instruments in the day-to-day operation of the company, they were of limited effectiveness.

On 11 October 1597 an amalgamated troupe of the Admiral's and Pembroke's men began playing at the Rose.[28] Initially Henslowe must have expected the company to function as it had previously, because he continued the same set of receipts that he had interrupted the previous July (f.27^v). Within ten days he added a new account by recording weekly income from the playhouse, commencing 21 October (f.36^v). For five days at the beginning of November he maintained both accounts, only to let the first drop altogether. The weekly record then continued until 4 March 1598.

Concurrently, on the page (f.37) facing the weekly receipts, he began a record of loans to Robert Shaw for the company. These commence on 23 October. As happened a year earlier, Henslowe seems to have regarded the loans as a temporary measure, for he carefully entered the personal debts of one of the actors, Thomas Downton, on the lower half of the same page. On the verso of the page (f.37^v), Henslowe began a list of repayments to commence 1 December, though in fact only one payment was entered. Whatever his expectation, the loans continued, and again Henslowe resorted to a temporary expedient. He skipped a space below the repayment entry, apparently to leave room for additional payments, and continued his list of loans. By

[28] The company functioned as a joint enterprise for no more than two or two and a half months, if at all. Henslowe records a loan to Robert Shaw "to by a boocke of yonge horton for the company of my lord admeralles men & my lord of penbrockes" on 5 November 1597 (f.37). When, however, he recopies this entry after 28 December it is listed under loans charged only against "my lord admeralles" players (f.43^v).

28 December he had reached the bottom of that page (f.37^v). The top half of the next page was already filled with entries from 1595 and 1597.[29] It is at this time that Henslowe and the company must have come to a far-reaching agreement, for Henslowe turned to an unused portion of the *Diary* (f.43^v), and started a systematic listing of company loans, recopying the entries that he had already made since 23 October.[30] He continued this new form of entry unchanged from 1597 through 1603.

In the majority of books on the Elizabethan theatre, the authors assume that Henslowe exercised control over the Admiral's men during these years. They frequently refer to the company as "his" company. Baldwin charges him, for example, with being a taskmaster who drives writers hard,[31] a view that has been restated in rather strong terms quite recently by Glynne Wickham in *Early English Stages*. "The story of Henslowe's dealings with authors, especially the system he employed of putting them so deeply into his debt as to be obliged to write for his company and no other is too well known to require restating."[32] I must demur. This picture assumes that Henslowe exercised operational control over production, and although such an assumption as this

[29] There are five sets of entries on folio 38: the first from 1595, the second, extending to the middle of the page, from before 12 December 1597, and two from 12 and 19 December for private loans to William Borne. Only the last one, quite short, is dated after 28 December on 24 February 1598.

[30] Compare ff.37-37^v with f.43^v. The entries on the latter page substantially duplicate those on the first two pages. The only significant discrepancy occurs in the first entry which is dated 23 October on f.37 and 21 October on f.43^v.

[31] T. W. Baldwin, *The Organization and Personnel of the Shakespearean Company* (Princeton, 1927), pp. 27-31.

[32] Wickham, II, p. 129. Also see n. 6 for Jenkins, p. 22. Wickham's view virtually repeats Fleay's charge made more than seventy years earlier; see F. G. Fleay, *A Chronicle History of the London Stage* (London, 1890), p. 117.

is widespread it is not necessarily well-founded. At the very least, it gives an exaggerated idea of Henslowe's role in theatrical affairs.

We can examine that role from two points of view. First, what in fact it actually was. Second, what tendencies it exhibited. In order to define the actual role, we must know how to treat the mass of loans listed after 1597. Many of them are personal loans to players and writers. These must be distinguished from the company loans, which are entered systematically in the *Diary*. The systematic entries indicate that Henslowe and the actors came to an agreement whereby he would advance money for the company and recoup it from time to time. Initially, it appears that both parties envisioned payments being made directly by the company to Henslowe. Later events, however, occasionally required Henslowe to resort to an arrangement whereby he took the actors' share of the galleries in recompense. Under this system the company accumulated heavy debts which Henslowe would periodically audit, with the concurrence of the actors. Whatever the false starts the system may have had, after 1597 it was no longer an improvised matter. Obviously, business warranted such an outlay on Henslowe's part. But how did he make his profit?

It is difficult to discern a system of interest charges in the company loans.[33] If Henslowe did charge interest, then it

[33] The *Diary* records only one indisputable instance where Henslowe charged interest for a theatrical loan. On 6 December 1602, acting for Worcester's company, he bought four cloaks at £4 a cloak "& for my forberance of my mony to a lowe me vs vpon euery clocke," bringing the total charged against the company to £17 (f.118). The straight interest per item thus came to 6¼ percent. The answer to whether or not Henslowe charged interest on personal loans is less easy to ascertain. The *Diary* provides no clear evidence that he did. However, in a preliminary investigation of Elizabethan financial practice, a stu-

must be buried in advances or payments to dramatists or tradesmen. But this is hard to uncover. Many of the payments for specific plays come to £6. This is the amount normally paid for a script. Nowhere, in all the entries involving advances to writers, is there a sign of a discounting procedure; therefore it is unlikely that the interest came out of the dramatist's £6. On the other hand, nothing is added to the company's debt beyond the outlay to the dramatist. We are forced to conclude that Henslowe did not enter into this new loan system in order to earn a banker's profit.

Unfortunately, since Henslowe abandoned his daily record of takings from the playhouse after 1597, we have no idea whether or not the new system brought him a larger share of the players' income. It might be appropriate at this juncture to wonder why Henslowe did not continue the daily record. My confessedly unfounded impulse is to associate this change also with Alleyn's retirement. If a daily report of income was needed before 1597 as a record for anyone but Henslowe, it is more likely to have been required for accounting with Alleyn than with the Master of the Revels, as Foakes and Rickert suggest,[34] since Henslowe's payments to the Master of the Revels were based on the number of weeks the playhouse was open rather than on the daily income of the players. My argument cannot be pressed too far, of course, for there is no evidence that Alleyn shared in the business affairs of the Rose before 1597, yet it is important to note that Alleyn and Henslowe

---

dent of mine, David Keller, has gathered evidence to show that the phrase "lawful money of England" was sometimes used to cover the loan of clipped or debased coins and repayment in whole coins. He suggests that the appearance of this phrase in the *Diary* (e.g., ff.12, 30) may indicate that Henslowe employed this subterfuge.

[34] Foakes and Rickert, p. xxix.

were in business at the Bear Garden from 1594 onward, and that the daily record for the Rose disappeared as soon as Alleyn retired from the company.

To return to my initial and fundamental query, if Henslowe did not earn interest or an increased share by advancing large sums to the company, what did he gain? I believe it was stability. He was guaranteeing continuous use of his playhouse through his loans. Before 1594 he had had an unsteady time of it. In 1597 he had lost a number of actors to Langley, and only good fortune had eliminated the competition. Not that he had planned to underwrite the players, but after their poor season of 1596, their loss of Alleyn's services, and then their failure to play at Court, the Admiral's men had to make valiant efforts to reestablish their position. The large sums supplied to Henslowe were used primarily to secure new plays as well as to add to the wardrobe of the company.

There still remains the question of control. At this time did Henslowe participate in approving plays, choosing costumes, and determining presentations? Was he instrumental in bringing certain playwrights together or in commissioning works? For an answer we must turn to the company-loan entries themselves.

Once Henslowe systematized advances to the company, he adopted several conventional modes of recording them. Most entries begin with the statement "lent unto" or "laid out for." Fewer, but still numerous, entries commence with the phrase "paid unto." The recipient is usually mentioned. Most frequently, he is one of the actors, so that the entry might read, for example, "Lent vnto Robart shawe the 26 of Janewarye [1599] to paye Thomas hawode in full payment for his boocke called ware [war] wth owt blowes & loue wthowt stryfe the some of ....xxxx^s" (f.53). Frequently, the recipient named might be the company itself as in the phrase "lent unto the company," "laid out for the company," or "paid unto" or "paid for" the company.[35] Finally, there are a number of entries that list direct payments or advances to dramatists or tradesmen without specifying that these monies were laid out either for the company or at the behest of its members.

I shall make a simple assumption. I shall assume that the different wording of these entries is not interchangeable, that each phrase reflects, as carefully as possible, the exact nature of a transaction. In particular, it seems to me, the matter of who authorized a loan, an advance, or a payment is significant. Did Henslowe make contracts on his own authority or at the behest of the company? Fortunately, as a supplement to the loan entries, several letters of authorization from the actors to Henslowe have survived. For example, we find the following entry in the *Diary* for 14 June 1600:

> pd vnto drayton hathway monday & deckers at the a poyntment of Robart shawe in full payment of A Boocke called the fayer constance of of [sic] Rome the 14 of June 1600 some of ....xxxxiiijs (f.69^v)

The authority for this payment lies in a letter from Shaw to Henslowe:

> I praye you Mr Henshlowe deliuer vnto the bringer hereof the some of fyue & fifty shilling^e to make the 3^{ll}-fyue shilling^e wch they receaued before, full six

---

[35] Some entries are recorded not as payments of loans but as receipts, viz., "Receaued by me Robt shaa [Shaw] of phillip Henslowe to pay H. Chettle. . ." (f.65). Only one such entry appears before 4 October 1599 (on 11 April 1598, f.46). Thereafter, this form appears with some frequency, the recipient of money usually being a member of the company, although sometimes a dramatist. My treatment of these entries is the same as for loans or payments.

pound^e in full payment of their booke Called the fayre
Constance of Roome.

But Henslowe gave them only 44s. Was he cheating? Shaw's
letter continues:

> whereof I pray you reserue for me Mr Willsons whole
> share wch is xjs. wch I to supply his neede deliuered hime
> yesternight.[36]

Presumably such a letter or possibly its oral equivalent
underlay each of those entries wherein Henslowe cited the
authority of either particular actors or the entire company.
These I shall term *authorized* payments.

Some entries, however, do not cite actors or company.
They record direct payment to dramatists or tradesmen, as
in the following entry:

> lent vnto m^r drayton the 24 of June 1598 in earneste of
> a boocke called the funerall of Richard cordelion the
> some of ....xxxs   (f.46^v)

Such entries I shall term *non-authorized*. On what basis
Henslowe made non-authorized loans or payments is hard
to say. He may have omitted a record of approval, though
I doubt that. Or they may reflect oral as distinct from written approval. Or, and we must allow this possibility, they
indicate independent action on Henslowe's part based on
his familiarity with company affairs. For instance, in a
series of entries concerning a particular play, one entry may
be authorized and another non-authorized, indicating that
the project as a whole is approved although a specific entry
may not have received company authorization.

Between 23 October 1597 and 12 March 1603, Henslowe

[36] Manuscripts, I, Article 31, printed in Foakes and Rickert, p. 294.
Also in *Papers*, pp. 55-56. I have followed Foakes and Rickert's tran-
scription. This letter is the only evidence of Wilson's part in the play.

recorded 341 entries covering payments to dramatists and the purchase of playscripts for the Admiral's men. Of this number, 16 concern a variety of purchases that do not involve direct payments to playwrights for new plays. That leaves 325 entries. Of these, 75 percent, or 244, are authorized, 81 non-authorized. [37] There is no question, then, that Henslowe infrequently advanced money not previously approved by the company. This point is further reinforced if we look at the distribution of these authorizations over a period of five and a half years. If we take the gross number of purchases for scripts, 341, the proportion of non-authorized to authorized entries year by year breaks down in the following manner: during 1597-98, 39 of 95 entries, or 41 percent, were non-authorized; in 1599, 21 percent were non-authorized; in 1600, 26 percent, in 1601, 20 percent, and in 1602-03, only 3 percent. This distribution indicates that Henslowe may have exercised or attempted to exercise independence in the early stages of the new agreement, but that with time he found that he could not do so effectively, or with time the company reasserted its full authority.

From this evidence—and the evidence from the purchase of costumes and properties is substantially the same[38]—it is patent that the kind of responsibility associated with a theatrical manager was not exerted by Henslowe at this time. Therefore, to write of him as a hard taskmaster who

[37] Even so high a figure as 81 for non-authorized plays is deceptive. These 81 entries cover outlays for 43 different plays. Of these 43 plays, 15 show no evidence of authorization in any other entries. Twelve of the plays are named also in authorized entries, but only on dates later than the initial non-authorized entry. For the remaining 16 plays, the first entry is authorized although one or more subsequent entries are non-authorized.

[38] Of 168 entries for costumes and properties, 147 were authorized and 18 were non-authorized. Three cannot be tabulated in this manner.

maintained ruthless control over a stable of writers, forcing them to turn out hack script after hack script, simply does not fit the facts. If the dramatists were driven to rapid composition and unhealthy collaboration, they were driven to it by the needs of the company and its willingness to advance money toward a future play. The advances were strictly limited, however. Not by Henslowe, but by the actors. As Greg pointed out long ago, the dramatist had to submit a certain number of pages in order to secure additional advances.[39] Increasingly, as we have seen, these advances were made not by Henslowe independently, but only on the authority of the company.

If, then, the role he played was strictly limited, did it exhibit tendencies that were never fully realized? Here I believe that scholars may be on firmer ground. The distribution of entries can be read in several different ways, one of which is that Henslowe sought to play a more independent role in the management of the company than in fact he was able to do. Early in 1598, on the leaf preceding the new entries (f.43), Henslowe began what seems to have been intended as a continuing investment: "A not[e] of all suche goods as I haue Bowght for [p]laynge sence my sonne edward allen leafte [p]laynge 1597." The first purchase is of a cloak, on 29 December. Thereafter, he made purchases on 18 April 1598, on an unrecorded date, and on 8 November. On 22 April 1599, he began a series of unrelated receipts below this last entry. I am led to conclude from this page that Henslowe intended to accumulate theatrical property but that in fact he purchased very little. In sum, I believe that Henslowe, finding himself dealing directly with the actors, sought to increase his influence in their affairs. But given the traditional organization of the acting company, there was no place for a business manager. We

39 Greg, *Diary*, II, p. 123.

must not underestimate the importance of Henslowe's investment in keeping the Admiral's men at the Rose. In this he may only have been imitating Langley who laid out £300 to prepare the Swan and to provide the players with "apparell fytt and necessarie for ther playeinge."[40] Knowingly or unknowingly, Henslowe was testing the traditional system, yet his outlays did not lead to control. If the capability of the Admiral's men to reduce their debt to £24 by 14 March 1604 (f.110) is any sign, the actors were able to keep their autonomy intact, at least temporarily.

The relation of Henslowe to the company becomes further complicated with the reentry of Edward Alleyn into theatrical affairs. Legend has it that Alleyn's return to the stage was commanded by the aging Queen. However true legend may be, his return coincides with the construction of a new playhouse, the Fortune. Despite the fact that the circumstances surrounding this construction are particularly well documented, Henslowe's part in it is somewhat difficult to unravel. There is no doubt that he was intimately connected with Alleyn in the venture. What is uncertain is his exact contribution.

On 22 December 1599 Patrick Brewe assigned his lease in certain property and buildings along Golding Lane to Edward Alleyn.[41] Less than three weeks later, Alleyn and Henslowe jointly entered into a contract with the builder of the Globe, Peter Streete, for the construction of the Fortune on that property.[42] Four days later, 12 January, the Lord Admiral issued a warrant to the justices and officers of Middlesex County authorizing the construction of the new theatre by Alleyn "and his Companye." Resistance to

---

[40] Langley's answer to the complaints brought against him by the players. *Shaw et al. v. Langley* in Wallace, p. 348.

[41] Muniment 20 printed in *Papers*, p. 15.

[42] Muniment 22 printed in *Papers*, pp. 4-7. Also available in Foakes and Rickert, pp. 306-310.

the new building arose, however, for sometime later the inhabitants of Finsbury petitioned the Privy Council to allow the playhouse as a benefit to the neighborhood. Finally, on 8 April, the Privy Council itself directed the justices to "permitt and suffer the said Edward Allen to proceede in theffectinge and finishinge of the same Newehowse."[43] This they apparently did, for throughout the spring and summer Peter Streete proceeded with construction. At this time Henslowe reappears. The records testify to the close watch that Henslowe kept over the project (ff.98^v-99). A fall-off in loans to the Admiral's men that summer and autumn indicates that the company was preparing to move to the Fortune. They ceased playing at the Rose by the end of October, and on 11 November Henslowe lent the company £4 "to paye vnto my sonne EAlleyn A bowt ther composicion" (f.70^v). In the next entry Henslowe recorded that he had "pd vnto my sonne alleyn for the firste weckes playe the xj parte of xvij^{li} ixs," or about 32s. Finally, on 4 April 1601, Alleyn executed a lease granting Henslowe a moiety in the playhouse and grounds together with a moiety of all income from playing and other sources.[44]

What are we to make of this sequence of events? Was the Fortune "entirely [Alleyn's] own adventure," as Greg states,[45] or was it a joint enterprise as Joseph Quincy Adams thinks,[46] or was it primarily Alleyn's venture in which "Henslowe was essentially in the position of a banker," as Patterson claims?[47] No one can be sure. I discern several interesting conjunctions. Alleyn alone took the lease on the land but he and Henslowe together entered into the build-

---

[43] Manuscripts, I, Articles 27-29, printed in Foakes and Rickert, pp. 288-291.

[44] Muniment 53 printed in *Papers*, p. 25.

[45] Greg, "Edward Alleyn," p. 22.   [46] J. Q. Adams, p. 267.

[47] Patterson, p. 229.

ing contract. Alleyn alone is mentioned in the Lord Admiral's and the Privy Council warrants and yet Henslowe seems to have been more closely involved in the day-to-day details of construction than Alleyn. The composition between the company and the landlord seems to have been with Alleyn alone, yet Henslowe was handling Alleyn's share of playhouse earnings. And at last, a year after the Privy Council warrant, Alleyn deeded a moiety of his interest in the playhouse and adjacent properties to Henslowe for a mere £8 a year. True, in later testimony Alleyn explained the low rental as *quid pro quo* for other quarters granted Alleyn by Henslowe.[48] Nonetheless, these contradictory conjunctions lead me to the following interpretation. It was not Henslowe but Alleyn who acted as banker or financier. He supplied a substantial part of the funds needed for construction. In addition, his reputation and standing served as the front for the enterprise, thus enabling the partnership to secure the warrants so necessary to success. The swiftness with which Alleyn and Henslowe moved, from leasing the land to eliciting the Lord Admiral's official support, a matter of twenty-two days, indicates pre-planning and coordination. Whether or not Alleyn once again took the lead, as he had done with the Bear Garden, we cannot know, but that Henslowe acted as the foreman in this scheme is evident enough. Alleyn, on the other hand, seems to have been no longer involved in the daily affairs of the company.

As J. P. Collier remarked more than a century ago, "It may be doubted whether Alleyn ever really liked his profession."[49] Although his last recorded performance, at

[48] Alleyn's Bill in *Alleyn v. Henslowe* (1624), printed in C. W. Wallace, "Three London Theatres of Shakespeare's Time," *The University Studies of the University of Nebraska* (Lincoln, 1909), pp. 338-339.

[49] J. Payne Collier, *Memoirs of Edward Alleyn* (London, 1841), p. 97.

a special ceremony to welcome King James to London, was
given on 13 March 1604, he may have ceased professional
playing earlier. His name does not appear in the company
list of February 1602 (f.104) nor did he act for the company
after 3 November 1602 (f.108). Yet the fact that he continued to receive Court payments for the company through
15 January 1604[50] suggests that he held a special position
among the players, possibly ceremonial in character. Perhaps he continued to perform only at Court, for he would
certainly want to establish himself with the new monarch.
Under those circumstances Henslowe would be likely to
handle the daily affairs of the Fortune.

Henslowe's *Diary* comes to a close in 1604. Its final entries
strongly suggest that an era was ending. The Admiral's
men, about to become the Prince's men, had reduced their
debt to £24 by 14 March 1604. Worcester's men, whom
Henslowe had funded from August 1602 to March 1603,
were about to become the Queen's men and would soon
move to the Red Bull Playhouse. In 1605 Henslowe's lease
of the Rose property came to an end. Terms for renewal
being unsatisfactory, he abandoned the playhouse, which
was torn down soon after.[51] In 1608 Alleyn and he seem to
have planned to lease shares in the Fortune Playhouse to
company members, just as the Burbage brothers had done
earlier with the Globe. It is doubtful, however, that they
ever pursued the plan.[52] With the end of the Fortune period, then, Henslowe's involvement in theatrical matters
became marginal for the next seven years. Instead, he and

[50] Chambers, IV, p. 168.

[51] In an order dated 25 April 1606 the Sewer Commission refers to
"the Late Playhouse in Maiden lane called the Rose." Quoted by Patterson, p. 241.

[52] Muniment 33 printed in *Papers*, pp. 13-14. Alleyn and Henslowe
prepared a lease for one thirty-second part of the Fortune to be issued
to Thomas Downton, the actor. The lease was never executed.

124938

Alleyn became increasingly active in the promotion of animal-baiting.

Alleyn alone purchased the Bear Garden in 1594, as I have stated already. There, Henslowe and he promoted the sport of baiting bears, bulls, and mastiff dogs on license from the then master, Ralph Bowes. From the beginning the partners intended to secure the mastership for the game for themselves, and thus save paying for the license. As Ralph Bowes lay ill in 1598, Henslowe made vigorous efforts to gain the office in reversion, but without success. The Queen granted the patent to John Dorrington, who held it until shortly after James came to the throne. On Dorrington's death, the partners were disappointed again. The King granted the mastership to Sir William Steward. Steward, knowing that Henslowe and Alleyn wanted the office for themselves, refused either to renew their former license or to buy out their investment,[53] thereby forcing them to purchase the mastership from him for £450. By patent dated 24 November 1604 Henslowe and Alleyn became joint masters. Although they later complained that they were at great charges in the purchase and were conducting the business at a minimal profit, they seemed to do well in the long run. Alleyn noted that he made £60 a year over the life of his investment, and Henslowe was quite content to purchase the Bear Garden from him in 1610.[54]

It may be that Henslowe's managerial talents had fuller scope in this business. Baiting had been a frequent entertainment at Court until 1588, after which, if the accounts are complete, it disappeared until 1599. Thereafter, exhibitions are reported yearly in the Council warrants. Henslowe makes his first appearance in those records in April 1604 as deputy to Dorrington. It was in this year, with

[53] Manuscripts, II, Article 9, printed in *Papers*, p. 104.
[54] Foakes and Rickert, p. 301.

the coming of James, that not only did the frequency of baiting exhibitions increase, but the nature of baiting took a novel turn. It appears to have been James himself who wished to test the mettle of the Tower lions by having them baited by mastiffs, and therefore, "the k. caused Edward Allen, late seruant to the Lord Admirall, now sworne the Princes man, and master of the Bear Garden, to fetch secretly 3. of the fellest dogs" to fight the lions.[55] This sport was repeated in subsequent years while other novelties were encouraged. As in the past, though Alleyn seems to have started a new enterprise, it was Henslowe who continued it. Between 1604 and 1614, it is his name that occurs most frequently in the council warrants, and although Alleyn still shared the mastership with Henslowe, he retired from active service until after Henslowe's death.

The last and perhaps most significant period of Henslowe's theatrical career, the Hope period, began in mid-1611. From his first known contact with the Lady Elizabeth's men, Henslowe's methods of operation differed from those he used a decade or more earlier. On 27 April 1611, John Townsend, Joseph Moore, and others received a patent as Lady Elizabeth's servants. Later that year, at the end of August, they gave bond to Philip Henslowe that they would fulfill the conditions agreed to in the articles. Although the articles are similar in character to the bonds given by individual actors in 1597, it is notable that here the entire company bound itself and, moreover, did so according to specified terms of employment. Unfortunately, the articles from this agreement do not survive, but in March 1613 Henslowe joined forces with Philip Rossiter to combine the Queen's Revels with the Lady Elizabeth's men. It is probable that this is the company, or its immediate successor,

---

[55] John Stow, *The Annales, or Generall Chronicle of England* continued by Edmond Howes (London, 1615), pp. 835-836.

that is the subject of Articles of Agreement between Henslowe and Jacob Meade, his former assistant and new partner, and the actor Nathan Field, representing the company.

The articles, probably dating from 1614, cover the usual three-year period.[56] They contain nine points, five dealing with obligations of the partners to supply means of production, one covering procedures for arbitrating disputes among actors, and three specifying the accounts due the company. A year or so later, considerable disagreement between Henslowe and the players arose over the issue of these accounts, the provisions of this agreement notwithstanding. But in 1614, more significant for Henslowe's emerging managerial influence were the points dealing with means of production. Henslowe and Meade assumed responsibility for supplying a playhouse and furnishing costumes and properties for the company whenever it played either in London or on tour. They further agreed to advance monies for the purchase of new plays, the repayment to come on the second or third day it is performed. At first glance these provisions do not seem so different in character from those that prevailed at the Rose and Fortune. Yet there is a subtle change. They stipulate that the purchase of stage furnishings and apparel as well as the advancement of funds for plays were to be made on the advice of "ffower or ffive Sharers of the saide Company *chosen* by the saide Phillipp and Jacob." Similarly, actors were to be removed from the company by Henslowe and Meade at the request of a majority of the company "*if* the saide Phillipp Henslowe and Jacob Meade shall fynde [the s]aide request to be just." Thus, in decisions concerning production materials, choice of play, and composition of

[56] Muniment 52 printed in *Papers*, pp. 23-25. For quotations below see lines 13, 31, 40-41 (Italics mine, B.B.).

the company, Henslowe and Meade were ceded an authoritative role in the operation of the company.

Concurrently, Henslowe pursued another line in securing a playhouse. In 1611, the one playhouse he had an interest in, the Fortune, was occupied by the Prince's men. The Bear Garden, which he now wholly owned, was not fit for theatrical performance. Therefore, he had to secure some other house for the Lady Elizabeth's men. It is generally supposed that he rented the Swan, and this may have been so. If it was indeed, then it was a temporary measure, for in the course of 1613 Henslowe decided upon an original solution to his problem. He would combine his need for a playhouse with his continuing use of a baiting ring. On 29 August 1613, he and Meade contracted with Gilbert Katherens to tear down the old Bear Garden and erect on its site a multipurpose building capable of housing both plays and sporting events.[57] The new playhouse, dubbed the Hope, was probably completed by the end of 1613, at which time the company moved to it.

Further insight into how Henslowe operated under the terms of the 1614 agreement comes from three sources. First, there survive other articles of agreement between the two theatrical partners and Robert Dawes, an actor whom they brought into the company against the wishes of the other sharers.[58] Second, there is extended correspondence between several dramatists, particularly Robert Daborne, and Henslowe. Daborne's correspondence starts 17 April 1613 and runs more than a year to 2 August 1614.[59] Third, there are articles of grievance against Henslowe drawn up

[57] Muniment 49 printed in *Papers*, pp. 19-22.

[58] *Papers*, pp. 123-125.

[59] Manuscripts, I, Articles 70-98, printed in *Papers*, pp. 67-83. The last letter, although dated 31 July 1614, contains a notation in Henslowe's hand dated 2 August 1614.

by the actors sometime after February 1615.[60] The charges, whether exaggerated or not, tell us much about Henslowe's later methods.

Both the Dawes articles and the articles of grievance show that crucial decisions concerning company organization and working conditions came to rest in Henslowe's hands. Since the articles of grievance attack Henslowe alone, we can assume that he was the controlling agent and that Meade continued to occupy a subordinate position in their theatrical affairs. The first part of the articles of grievance records instances between March 1612 and February 1615 when Henslowe allegedly appropriated funds or goods to his own use without giving due credit to the company. According to the actors, Henslowe owes them £567. The second part generalizes the instances of the first. Labeled "Articles of oppression against Mr: Hinchlowe," the second part specifies nine charges, six covering Henslowe's misappropriation of goods and funds, manipulation of hired personnel, and unjustified reservation of playbooks. The remaining three charges claim that Henslowe deliberately sought to maintain control over the players by keeping them in debt, requiring exorbitant bonds, and breaking companies at will, having "dissmembred five Companies" in three years. Without Henslowe's reply, it is hazardous either to accept or to reject these accusations. It is easy enough to regard Henslowe as a villain, a temptation to which many historians have succumbed, yet it is unnecessary to posit his guilt in order to recognize the reasons for these charges. Unquestionably, Henslowe sought to extend his control over company operation. As long as he himself did not hold a royal patent, he had to function through an approved troupe. The articles of

[60] Manuscripts, I, Article 106, printed in *Papers*, pp. 86-90.

grievance testify to the running battle between an increasingly dependent acting profession and an increasingly assertive theatrical investor. By making the hired men responsible to him, by adding actors to the company at his will, by retaining the stock of costumes and furnishings, and finally by requiring large bonds, Henslowe was able, if illegitimately so, to assume functions that only in years to come would legitimately accrue to a theatrical manager.

Together with exercising control over the actors, Henslowe seems to have established a direct authority over the writers. Their numbers had appreciably diminished since the 1590's. During 1613-14, only Robert Daborne, Nathan Field, Cyril Tourneur, Philip Massinger, Ben Jonson, and possibly John Fletcher seem to have been providing plays for the company.[61] Since the first four are linked together as collaborators in the Daborne correspondence as well as in letters from Field to Henslowe, it is reasonable to conclude that the theatrical conditions Daborne described for himself also prevailed for these other writers. Aside from the querulous bargaining that permeates the letters, Daborne's correspondence reveals the inroads that Henslowe had made in controlling the source and selection of plays for the company.

Three critical issues are involved in the relationship among dramatist, player, and investor. Who commissions a dramatic work? Who reads and approves it? Who controls the rights? A decade earlier one could have answered unequivocally "the company" to all these questions. But Daborne's correspondence shows that Henslowe had begun to commission plays, at least from Daborne, even supplying

[61] Appended to a letter from Nathan Field to Henslowe, probably written in 1613, is a sentence by Daborne referring to "the play of Mr ffletcher & owrs" (*Papers*, p. 66). This is the only reference to Fletcher in the correspondence.

him with a subject or book to dramatize.[62] The company seems to have continued to read and perhaps approve the copy of a play, yet Daborne gave a prior reading to Henslowe and Mr. Alleyn and seems to have taken for granted that Henslowe's approval was the significant approval.[63] Finally, Henslowe seems to have retained control over the playbooks. Daborne refers to giving parts rather than an entire script to the actors, a fact that squares with the actors' claim that Henslowe retained books belonging to them.[64] Thus, instead of merely advancing money for plays, as called for in the articles of agreement, Henslowe commissioned works, approved or disapproved copy, and then retained the rights to the final drafts. He may have engaged in the regular purchase and resale of scripts. In one instance at least, Daborne sold a play to Henslowe, though the players were clamoring for it, and suggested that Henslowe could resell it to the company at a profit.[65] As he had not done in previous years when he laid out money on the authorization of the players, Henslowe now acted independently, thus forcing the players to deal with the dramatists through him.

At this point, a question may well be raised: May not the conditions of the Hope period have been identical with those of the Rose, the only difference being that Daborne's letters give us access to a type of information not readily forthcoming from the earlier account? I think not. I think that we can be reasonably sure that we are indeed dealing with a changing theatrical situation rather than a variation in evidence. For instance, in 1597 the bonds between the actors and Henslowe were individual, purely formal, and

---

[62] Articles 73, 91 printed in *Papers*, pp. 69, 79.

[63] Articles 74, 75, 92, 94, 96 printed in *Papers*, pp. 69, 70, 80-82.

[64] Article 81 printed in *Papers*, pp. 73-74.

[65] Article 91 printed in *Papers*, p. 79.

Pages from Philip Henslowe's Diary

Comparison of f. 22v (Plate I) and f. 23 (Plate II).

Before October 1596 Henslowe had entered instalment sales of cloth to Jones (I:1-8) and a cloak to Maget (II:1-10). In mid-October of 1596 he commenced loans to the players (II:11-14), squeezing in the initial date of October 14 some-time later (II:15). On 29 October he began the entries for repayments lower on the page (II:26) much as he did with the sales listed at the top of the page. Some-time before the end of November he was forced to squeeze in a loan entry on f. 23 (II:24-25) and then carry over the account to the middle of the opposite page (I:13). Subsequent loans follow, mainly in December 1596 (I:21-28). In January Henslowe noted four substantial repayments at the bottom of f. 23 (II:30-36). As he entered the loans on f. 22v, he maintained a running total of the company debt (I:24-25, 29, 31). On 14 March he crammed in a last loan for the purchase of silks for *Guido* (I:32-33). A fortnight later, on 25 March, Henslowe noted an additional cash loan to the players and a summary of their outstanding account in the space left above the loans (I:9-12).

Comparison of f. 43v (Plate III), f. 37 (Plate IV), and f. 37v (Plate V).

Henslowe began a series of loans to the players on 23 October 1597 (IV:1). On 12 November, in the middle of the page, he began entries of personal loans to the actor, Thomas Downton (IV:17). These loans are written horizontally and systematically in comparison to the more haphazard entries to the company. On 1 December 1597 he squeezed in a company loan entry on f. 37 (IV:15-16) and commenced a note for repayments on the next page, f. 37v (V:1-3). On 8 December he carried the company loan entries over from f. 37 to 37v (V:4). On 28 December 1597 the next page is already filled with entries from 1595. He therefore turned ahead to f. 43v and commenced a systematic accounting of the company's loans. At the head of the page he described the account as money laid out for the Lord Admiral's men beginning 11 October 1597 (III:1-5) and then copied the entries inserted on f. 37 and f. 37v. The pages match in the following manner:

Plate III	Plate IV	Plate III	Plate V	Plate III	Plate V
6-8	1-5	17-20	4-9	32-33	24-25
9-11	6-10	21-22	10-11	34-35	26-28
12-14	11-14	23-26	12-16		
15-16	15-16	27-29	17-21		
		30-31	22-23		

The last entry on f. 43v (III:35-36) continues the loans.

Tate Wilkinson

contained no reference to other obligations beyond playing at the Rose. There is no sign that Henslowe interfered with the internal operations at that time. As for his dealings with dramatists between 1597 and 1603, there is abundant illustration that the company, not Henslowe, exercised control. Surviving letters from actors to Henslowe authorizing payments to writers, already cited, show that he acted on company directives. It was the company and not Henslowe who bound Chettle to write for the Lord Admiral's men in 1602 (f.105). And when it came to a dramatist's reading his play, he did so to the entire company and not to Henslowe alone (f.105^v). True, Henslowe showed an inclination toward extending his authority during periods of crisis, but his success in doing so was curtailed by 1604. Ten years later, in dealing with a new company and functioning as a senior partner, he was engaged in a more or less open struggle to wrest governing authority from the players.

We have now reached a point where we can assess Henslowe's role in theatrical production. In doing so, we need to distinguish the historical meaning of his position from its personal style.

Historically, Henslowe represented the manager of the future at an early stage of development. Yet his ability to function as a manager or producer was blocked by the structure of the acting company. In fact, the two could not co-exist. Shared responsibility among working actors not only followed different procedures of decision-making but had no room for managerial guidance. The company needed financing but not control and, in fact, resisted control by any single individual. Even an investment could not be adequately protected because that would have involved making artistic decisions about choice of repertory, engagement of actors, types of furnishings, and a thousand other details. Thus, all the theatrical investors who were not themselves theatre people suffered frustration in their theatrical dealings. John Brayne, Francis Langley, and even Philip Henslowe could create opportunities but could not control the actors' use of them. Consciously or not, Henslowe recognized, even before 1600, the fundamental enmity between management and company, and attempted to expand his role as landlord into that of manager. His withdrawal from active participation in the theatre during the first decade of the seventeenth century and his immersion in Bear Garden affairs resulted from his inability to breach the system of sharers. Why matters changed in 1611 is hard to say. Perhaps the shortage of playhouses, what with the razing of the Rose and the occupancy of all other theatres, may have driven the newly formed Elizabeth's men into Henslowe's hands. This time, however, he succeeded in forcing his way into company operations. By gradually making actors and writers responsible to him rather than to the company, he took the first step toward genuine management. But the days of the manager would not arrive until a generation later, when Thomas Killigrew and Sir William Davenant rather than the actors would receive patents to raise and maintain theatrical companies.

Henslowe's difficulties as well as his opportunities throughout his career owe a great deal to Edward Alleyn. His alliance with Alleyn enabled him to become intimately involved with the actors in a way not open to Langley, for example. But in the 1590's Henslowe could not take advantage of that intimacy, given the unity of the company and his lack of theatrical credentials. Only Alleyn could have bridged the gap between owner and performer in the way that Richard Burbage did for the Chamberlain's men. But Alleyn's interest did not lie in that direction. After 1597 he seems to have participated in company affairs only reluctantly. This was unfortunate. He was an enterprising man as well as a great actor. In instance after instance, it is he who initiated, or seems to have initiated, projects for the Henslowe-Alleyn partnership. Both the force of his personality and the range of his theatrical experience placed him in a position to have a decisive impact upon theatrical development. Unfortunately, his impact was negative. His popularity as an actor and his honored place in the company rendered the other actors dependent upon him, on one hand; on the other, his evident lack of commitment to the theatre weakened the company and made it vulnerable to managerial interference. Occasionally, force of personality can overcome history. Alleyn may have had such force, and theatrical history would have been different had he devoted his talents and energies to the theatre rather than to his philanthropic pursuits, such as the College of God's Gift at Dulwich. By contrast, Henslowe did not have such force, and therefore his activities reflected the play of events more than the surge of his will.

In assessing Henslowe's personal style then, we are bound to recognize how prosaic it was. True, Henslowe stands—and deserves to stand—in the line of those who have won a place in theatrical history through their business acumen. Indeed, he may justly be regarded as the first of that line in the English-speaking theatre. Yet his significance does not stem from unusual personal or intellectual qualities so much as from commonplace diligence. He typifies the reasonably able, reasonably decent businessman of the Elizabethan age, one who discovered, partly on his own initiative, largely through his connection with Alleyn, that theatre could be a profitable venture. He took advantage of the opportunities that occurred, but did not create opportunities out of mere possibilities. Responsive to circumstances, his career paralleled and thrived on the erosion of the players' autonomy. Neither in commercial organization nor in theatrical production, however, did Philip Henslowe exert an enduring influence that would mark him as the first true theatre manager in England.

One of God Almighty's Unaccountables
Tate Wilkinson of York

CHARLES BEECHER HOGAN

O^{N AN OCTOBER} afternoon in 1758 Tate Wilkinson, a young man of nineteen who the previous year had made his first appearance as an actor, sat at dinner in the house near Pall Mall in London of a certain Mrs. Wier. Another of Mrs. Wier's guests was an elderly gentleman named Joseph Baker. The accidental meeting of these two men was, said the younger, "the whole and sole occasion of bringing about my being manager."[1]

Now, Joseph Baker was, and had been for some fifteen years, the manager of a celebrated provincial theatre situated in the city of York. In the period I am discussing there had come into being throughout the British Isles a vast number of theatres such as that directed by Baker, which, when taken in the aggregate, can be considered almost as important as the three great London playhouses then in existence: Drury Lane, Covent Garden, and the Haymarket. There were, in fact, by the close of the eighteenth century, a greater number of provincial theatres than there are today. I have made a fairly exhaustive survey of this matter, and can report that in 1800 this number was exactly one hundred fifty, of which seventeen had been granted patents by the crown, and could therefore, like the London theatres, call themselves Theatres Royal. All of them were real

---

[1] Tate Wilkinson, *Memoirs of His Own Life*, 4 vols. (York, 1790), II, pp. 5-6, cited below as *Mem*. Wilkinson's other autobiographical work, *The Wandering Patentee; or, A History of the Yorkshire Theatres, from 1770 to the Present Time*, 4 vols. (York, 1795), is cited as *WP*. See also n. 50.

theatres: structures erected solely for the performance of plays. And in small towns, and even in large ones, there were literally hundreds of derelict churches or assembly rooms or town halls that were repeatedly being turned into temporary places of entertainment.

Entertainment is a large word: opera, circus, concert, vaudeville, ballet. My concern, however, is with theatres where plays were played and theatres where managers managed. Let me therefore return to my remark as to the aggregate importance of these country playhouses.

In the eighteenth century all theatres were strictly and uninterruptedly operated on the repertory system, and until well into the nineteenth they continued to be so. This meant that each theatre had a resident, and more or less permanent, company of actors, singers, dancers, house servants of all descriptions—and, most notably, a manager. The manager whose fortunes I shall presently review was in charge of no less than six playhouses. He lived two hundred miles from London, and it is obvious that a considerable number of his patrons very rarely, if ever, visited the metropolis. Hence he was under a particular obligation to bring forward such entertainment, as indeed would any astute manager, which would most likely keep his houses full.

But he was thoroughly conscious of a constant and pressing problem. A high percentage of his actors, especially if they were young, held fast to the dream of what might be awaiting them in London. As he once said, "We little curs must submit to [the London managers'] strong *bow wows*"[2] in enticing their players to Drury Lane or to Covent Garden. These country theatres, sometimes even the least important among them, had, then, a secondary value. They were training grounds. They were schools where perform-

2 *WP*, II, p. 247.

ers learned not only the art of acting but, too, such essential matters as the enormous number of parts in the plays that were in stock in every theatre of the British Isles.

Again, these theatres, especially in the last thirty or forty years of the eighteenth century, performed a more or less reverse function. Drury Lane and Covent Garden, the so-called "winter" theatres of London, were in general closed between May and September. To actors there is only one true happiness in life: that of acting. To actors, as to all of us, a pocket full of shillings has an advantage over a pocket filled only with halfpennies. Therefore, a very large number of established London players were repeatedly setting off for country engagements in the summer holiday. Throughout her professional career, from 1782 to 1812, Mrs. Siddons, for example, visited forty-three provincial theatres, from Belfast to Margate, from Glasgow to Plymouth.

These theatres were not invariably operated by and for themselves alone. Several country managers, that is, turned to the profitable device of broadening their activities to include, as I have already mentioned, as many as six different cities, or indeed even more. Theatrical circuits, as they were called, were to be found in Norfolkshire, in Kent, in south Wales, in Devonshire, and elsewhere. It is to the most famous of all the circuits of the late eighteenth century, located far in the north of England, that I now invite attention.

YORK, LEEDS, Wakefield, Pontefract, Doncaster, Hull. A small corner, indeed, of Yorkshire's 6,000 square miles, being a circuit of but some one hundred forty miles, but this was the domain over which the young man who had so fortunately agreed to be at dinner with Mrs. Wier eventually came to rule as, in his own words, "*sole* monarch."[3]

3 *WP*, I, p. 72.

Tate Wilkinson had never forgotten his fellow guest at that dinner. When, therefore, Wilkinson came to York as a strolling player in 1763 his first concern was to present himself at Joseph Baker's door. Their friendship ripened swiftly; they became as father and son. Wilkinson acted at Baker's theatre for a few weeks, but then, with a youthful restlessness, he went journeying elsewhere: to London, Shrewsbury, Dublin, and many other cities. But York and Baker's affectionate solicitude brought him repeatedly northward, and when Baker died in 1770 it was his dearest wish that his son Tate should assume the theatre's leadership.

Wilkinson fell in love with York. He states that he would not change his situation there "for the management of any other theatre in the world,"[4] it being his "favourite study, happiness and pride."[5] In 1803 Charles Mathews, one of his most eminent pupils, left Yorkshire for a highly successful first appearance at the Haymarket in London. Wilkinson wrote his congratulations. It was, he said, a feather not in Mathews' cap, but "in the cap of the York company."[6]

Under his guidance, beneficent, intelligent, and, as he himself well knew, eccentric, this company became (with the possible exception of the theatre at Bath) the provincial stage on which all fledgling performers and all seasoned performers—Kemble, Fawcett, Mrs. Siddons, Dodd, Mrs. Yates, and many others—most wished to be seen.[7] Of opportunities under Tate Wilkinson's management the actor John Bernard wrote in 1777, "every actor was talking."[8] It was Tate Wilkinson who in 1769, the third country manager

---

4 *WP*, II, p. 85.   5 *WP*, III, p. 226.

6 Mrs. [Anne] Mathews, *Memoirs of Charles Mathews*, 4 vols. (London, 1838-39), I, p. 406.

7 *WP*, III, p. 225.

8 John Bernard, *Retrospections of the Stage*, 2 vols. (London, 1830), I, p. 151.

in England to do so, bought at a personal expenditure of
£500[9] royal patents for York and for Hull, those documents
so essential to the dignity and the protection of the
comedians privileged to style themselves "His Majesty's
Servants." Over his entire company of players and over all
his theatres Tate Wilkinson's consuming love for his profession—he being, as he says, "bit by a theatrical tarantula"[10]—
spread like sunshine.

The principal one of these theatres was, of course, at
York itself. To the importance in history of this illustrious
and beautiful city I do not need to refer. In Wilkinson's day,
with its population of some 15,000 persons,[11] York could
scarcely be called a metropolis. But its strategic location on
the highway to Scotland has long been recognized, lying as
it does almost exactly halfway between London and Edinburgh. To a provincial theatre York's ease of access was
therefore a matter of high importance to its manager. This
he did not fail to take advantage of: a fact to which his two
long, loquacious, and valuable books of autobiography—to
a discussion of which I shall presently return—so many
times make reference.

A word, then, as to the venue of Wilkinson's most
important activities. In York at the present time the Theatre
Royal, as it is still called (even though the day of issuing
patents has long gone by), is situated almost exactly on the
same site as a theatre erected by one of Joseph Baker's
predecessors two hundred twenty-five years ago, in the summer, that is, of 1744. Baker remodeled this building, Wilkinson again remodeled it, and it has been frequently remodeled in later years. The topography of the city, at least
in that immediate area, has also undergone since the eighteenth century considerable changes. The modern theatre

9 *WP*, I, p. 73.   10 *Mem.*, I, p. 217.
11 *A New Description of York*, anon. (York, 1830), p. 4.

now fronts on St. Leonard's Place, which was constructed in the early 1830's. But the exterior of Wilkinson's theatre fronted on nothing; it was never visible to him or to anybody else. It stood completely surrounded by other buildings, one of which was Wilkinson's own dwelling in which was his dressing room with immediate access to the stage of the theatre.[12]

Its patrons walked to it from the northern end of Blake Street (at that time the theatre's customary address) through an alleyway which, states a playbill of March 1778, would the following winter "be commodiously cover'd into the street." What these patrons saw when they entered the auditorium we do not know; no likeness of it, possibly because none was ever executed, has survived. But we learn from a survey made in 1809[13] that in addition to the pit, where places were 2s. a ticket, it contained two tiers of boxes at 3s. a seat, a first gallery at 1s.6d., and an upper gallery at 1s. Over the proscenium, as Wilkinson took pains to boast, was "the most elegant *royal arms* . . . of any theatre in his Majesty's dominions."[14] On 3 August 1786 Mrs. Siddons acted in York to what Wilkinson states to be the greatest receipt ever recorded in that city, being £192.9s.6d.,[15] from which I have hazarded a guess that the theatre could hold some 550 spectators.

But Mrs. Siddons was not in a position to act at York every night of the season. It chances that one of Wilkinson's manuscript account books for the year 1784 is currently in the possession of the York City Library. What it reveals is the melancholy fact that the average nightly income from the sale of tickets at the door of the theatre was in the

---

12 *WP*, III, p. 172.
13 *A Description of York*, anon. (York, 1809), p. 69.
14 *Mem.*, IV, p. 143.
15 *Yorkshire Magazine*, I (August, 1786), p. 255.

For the BENEFIT of

Mrs. COLLINS.

THEATRE-ROYAL,

TUESDAY Evening, *April* 15, 1777,
Will be prefented a TRAGEDY, call'd

The Grecian Daughter.

EVANDER, Mr. WILKINSON.
PHILOTAS, Mr. BEYNON.
MELANTHON, Mr. ORAM.
PHOCION, Mr. RAYMUR.
ARCAS, Mr. HUDSON.
Greek Herald, Mr. BUCK. | *Greek Soldier*, Mr. COLBY.
CALLIPUS, Mr. EYLES.
DYONISIUS, Mr. CUMMINS.
ERIXENE, Mrs. EYLES.
The *GRECIAN DAUGHTER*,

By Mrs. SIDDONS,

Her Firft APPEARANCE on this STAGE.

By Particular DESIRE, A HORNPIPE
By a CHILD only Nine Years of Age. His fecond Appearance.

An ADDRESS to the TOWN,
By Mifs COLLINS.

Between the PLAY and FARCE, A *Paftoral Interlude*, call'd

The COUNTRY COURTSHIP.

ALEXIS, Mr. WOOD. | *DORUS*, Mr. BAKER.
PASTORA, Mifs SIMSON.

To which will be added an ENTERTAINMENT, call'd
THE

JUBILEE.

The SONGS and CHORUSSES, by Meffrs. WOOD, WHEELER, SUETT,
BAKER, and HUDSON.
Mrs. HUDSON, Mrs. MIELL, Mifs SIMSON, Mrs. LENG, &c.

Act 2d, A GRAND PAGEANT.
In which the Whole Company will walk in the different Characters of *Shakefpear*.
(With ALTERATIONS and ADDITIONS.)

The Monument Scene of ROMEO and JULIET.

To conclude with a New TRANSPARENCY of Shakefpear,
Attended by the TRAGIC and COMIC MUSES.
TRAGIC MUSE, Mrs. HUDSON. | *COMIC MUSE*, Mifs HOLMES.
With a ROUNDELAY.

To begin at Half paft Six o'Clock·

TICKETS as ufual, and of Mrs. COLLINS, at Mrs. *Hawkfworth's, Stonegate.*

Mrs. Siddons's first appearance at York, when Wilkinson states that he
"had the honour of being her old father." In later years Mrs. Siddons played
at York on seven different occasions.

(Never Acted Here.)
(Positively for this NIGHT ONLY.)
For the BENEFIT of
Mr. WILKINSON.

THEATRE-ROYAL.

EASTER TUESDAY Evening, APRIL 21, 1778,

Will be presented a NEW COMEDY, call'd THE

SCHOOL

FOR

SCANDAL.

It is almost needless to inform the Public of the unprecedented Success of the above COME-DY, not only in *London*, but at the Theatres-Royal in *Dublin* and *Bath*. It cannot, however, on any Consideration, be acted after this Night. The Public may depend upon Mr. WILKINSON's strict Attention in Regard to the Representation; and that not any Expence or Care will be wanting to render it worthy the Approbation of the Audience, and no Way injurious to the Credit of the very ingenious Author.

Sir PETER TEAZLE, Mr. W I L K I N S O N.
Sir OLIVER SURFACE, Mr. I N C H B A L D.
JOSEPH SURFACE, Mr. W A D D Y.
Sir BENJAMIN BACKBITE, Mr. K E N N E D Y.
CRABTREE, Mr. S U E T T.
MOSES, Mr. B U C K.
SNAKE, Mr. L E N G. | CARELESS, Mr. B U T L E R.
Sir TOBY, Mr. W O O D. | TRIP, Mr. B E Y N O N.
ROWLY, Mr. O R A M.
CHARLES SURFACE, Mr. C U M M I N S.

Mrs. CANDOUR, Mrs. T A P L I N.
Lady SNEERWELL, Mrs. I N C H B A L D.
MARIA, Miss M U C K L O W.
Lady TEAZLE, Miss H O L M E S.

With NEW SCENES, DECORATIONS, &c.

After which will be *reviv'd* a MUSICAL ENTERTAINMENT of three Acts, call'd THE

SUMMER's TALE.

A NEW OVERTURE to the Entainment, compos'd by Mr. SHAW.
BELLAFONT, Mr. W O O D.
FREDERICK, Mr. B U T L E R.
Sir ANTHONY WITHERS, Mr. I N C H B A L D.
AMELIA, Mrs. L E N G.
MARIA, Mrs. H I T C H C O C K.

TICKETS at the usual Places, and of Mr. WILKINSON a the Theatre.
BOX, 3 s.—PIT, 2 s.—First GAL. 1 s. 6 d.—Upper GAL. 1 s.

N. B. Mr. WILKINSON being honour'd with a very extraordinary Demand for Places, requests the Ladies will send their Servants at Half past Five to prevent Confusion or any Mistakes.—Doors open'd at Five.

The School for Scandal was first acted at Drury Lane on 8 May 1777. Mrs. Inchbald, later well known as a dramatist, was a member of Wilkinson's company from 1777 to 1780.

At the THEATRE in WAKEFIELD,

On WEDNESDAY Evening, October 21, 1778, will be presented,

A COMEDY called The

RECRUTING OFFICER.

CAPTAIN PLUME, Mr KEMBLE,

(His first Appearance on this Stage)

Serjeant Kite, Mr INCHBALD.
Worthy, Mr BUTLER.
Justice Ballance, Mr ORAM.
Bullock, Mr BUCK.
Justice Scale, Mr LENG.
Two Recruits, Mr SUETT and Mr COLBY.
Welch Collier, Mr HASKER.
Captain Brazen, Mr KING.

Rose, Mrs HITCHCOCK.
Melinda, Mrs CUMMINS.
Lucy, Mrs LENG.
Collier's Wife, Miss MOORE.
Sylvia, Mrs INCHBALD.

To which will be added a Pantomime Entertainment, (the last Time) called The

WIZARD:

OR, THE

Adventures of HARLEQUIN.

The Scenery and Machinery entirely New; particularly the Grocer's Shop, the Hotel, the Garden, Temple, Silver Rocks, Cascade, &c. &c.

Harlequin, Mr COLBY.
Pantaloon, Mr BUCK.
Wizard, Mr WOOD.
Clown, Mr SUETT.

Mother, Mrs LENG.
Colombine, Miss MOORE.

To begin at a Quarter past Six o'Clock.

‡§† TICKETS——BOX, 3s. PIT, 2s. GALL. 1s. to be had at *Haigh's* Music-shop; the *Black-Bull*; Mr *Meggitt's*; and at the *Printing-Office.*

Places to be taken of Mr Hitchcock, at the Theatre, from Ten to One.

On this night John Philip Kemble acted to a house of £12. He was to remain with Wilkinson until 1781, when he accepted an engagement at Dublin.

To the PUBLIC.

A Gentleman of Taſte and Experience in the Theatrical World, having mentioned to Mr. WILKINSON that he intended giving an Evening's Entertainment at a LONDON THEATRE, under the Title of "HUMOURS and PASSIONS; or, The SCHOOL of SHAKESPEARE"—Mr. W. hought ſuch a Plan might be agreeable to the Stage to take Piece-Meal, eſtabliſhed Stock Plays, for the Purpoſe, ſuch as The MERCHANT of VENICE, HAMLET, HENRY VIII. OTHELLO, &c. &c. but is of Opinion, and humbly ſubmits to the Public, if he could bring forward detached Acts from SHAKESPEARE, MASSINGER, and others, where the greateſt Beauties may be found, and from ſuch Plays as are entirely, or in a great Meaſure, loſt to the Stage, it would be affording a nouvelle and inſtructive Amuſement for one Night's Performance. As for Inſtance: The Third Act of JULIUS CÆSAR, by SHAKESPEARE, may be averred equal to any Play he ever wrote: but the Laſt Act, performed even by the beſt Actors, cannot 'claim Attention, and requires great Care to prevent Laughter. The ſame may be ſaid of "The WINTER'S TALE, and TAMING of the SHREW, yet both are made excellent Pieces, in Three Acts, by Mr. GARRICK.—LOVE'S LABOUR LOST; the Three Plays of HENRY VI. TROILUS and CRESSIDA; ANTONY and CLEOPATRA; RICHARD II. &c. notwithſtanding they ſhare, in particular Scenes, the Fire and maſterly Strokes of his wonderful Pen, equal to the beſt of his Works; yet, on the whole, are ſo little calculated for Stage Effect at preſent, that moſt of thoſe mentioned may be pronounced as entirely confined to the Cloſet, unleſs by the Means here propoſed.——He therefore intends the following as a Specimen, which, if accepted, and honoured with the Approbation of the Audience, there is a Fund of Entertainment in Store, that may be collected in the ſame Manner from ſeveral obſolete Authors.

(The Laſt Week of the Company's Performing this Seaſon.)

THEATRE-ROYAL, *YORK*,
On TUESDAY Evening, MAY 1, 1781,
Will be preſented,

A SELECTED ENTERTAINMENT,
TAKEN FROM
Shakeſpeare, Maſſinger, and Dr. Young,
INTITLED

Humours & Paſsions
OR,
A THEATRICAL FETE.
IN SEVERAL DIVISIONS;
The FIRST from SHAKESPEARE's

JULIUS CÆSAR.

** From the *Playhouſe Companion*, Vol. I. "The Speeches of *Brutus* and *Antony* over *Ceſar's* Body are perhaps the fineſt PIECES of ORATORY in the Engliſh Language. The Firſt appearing unanſwerable till the Second comes to overthrow its Effect."

BRUTUS, Mr. WILKINSON.
ARTEMIDORUS, Mr. WOOD.
LUCIUS, Maſter HITCHCOCK. | Octavius's Servant, Mr. HASKER;
PLEBEIANS, Mr. BAILEY, Mr. COLBY, Mr. HITCHCOCK; Mr. TYLER, &c.
MARC ANTONY, Mr. CUMMINS.
PORTIA, Mrs. SMITH.

SECOND DIVISION taken from MASSINGER's

ROMAN ACTOR.
[WITH DECORATIONS, &c.]

Playhouſe Companion: "This Play was conſidered by its Author, and by other Dramatic Poets, his Cotemporaries, to have been the moſt perfect Work of his *Minerva*, as appears from his own Epiſtle Dedicatory, and by no leſs than ſix ſeveral Copies of Verſes prefixed to it. It could *not*, therefore, fail of meeting with Succeſs in the Repreſentation. It was revived with ſome Alterations, and printed in 1722, in Five Acts; and even before that time Mr. *Betterton* occaſioned it to be got up, and gained great Applauſe in the Part of the *Roman Actor* which he himſelf performed. The Plot of it may be found in the Hiſtorians of the Reign of *Domitian*, and the Scene lies at *Rome*."

In this DIVISION will be

A Defence of the Stage,

By *Paris*, the *Roman Actor*, in Anſwer to an Accuſation brought againſt it before the *Senate*.

PARIS, (the Roman Actor) Mr. KEMBLE.
RUSTICUS, Mr. TYLER. | SURA, Mr. COLBY. | PARTHENIUS, Mr. HITCHCOCK.
LICTORS, Mr. WOOD, Mr. LENG, Mr. BAILEY, Mr. CHALMERS, and Others.
ARETINUS, Mr. SMITH. | Æsopus, Mr. INCHBALD. | LATINUS, Mr. HASKER.

Wilkinson here remarks on certain plays by Shakespeare that are "little calculated for Stage Effect." He takes care, however, to add "at present."

neighborhood of £20—with nightly expenditures of 20 guineas—and that on one disastrous evening it was no more than £4.2s. The consequence was that Wilkinson at the very outset of his career took refuge in soliciting his public to purchase season tickets by subscription.[16] It was a practice he was obviously obliged to continue without interruption. In that year, 1784, he had subscriptions totaling £155.12s. These tickets, averaging about £14 a night,[17] were a modest assistance to the little nonsubscription £4 just mentioned. But oftentimes it was uphill work.

In his books he speaks on many occasions of what no manager in history has ever been able to avoid. "My troops [at York] were not in a flourishing state by any means."[18] At Leeds "all our golden dreams were frustrated."[19] "My nights that year [at Hull], as manager, were very thinly attended."[20] As to this circumstance Wilkinson advances, in the light of his circuit being a provincial one, two suggestions that seem to be valid. One is the insistence of supercilious busybodies living in York and elsewhere in the country who pretended to have entire knowledge of what is good or bad in all matters relating to the stage. Their manifestoes gained the ears of the credulous or the illiterate, and the result for the manager is £4.2s. Another reason (and this was written in 1790) was the improved condition of the highway between London and York. A playgoer visited Drury Lane on Wednesday night, left town on Thursday, and was in York by Saturday noon. Why should he attend the theatre there to see the same play he saw three nights ago, acted and produced by better actors and with better scenery?[21]

There are many qualities in Tate Wilkinson that interest

16 *WP*, II, pp. 212-228.   17 *WP*, II, p. 216.
18 *WP*, II, p. 88.   19 *WP*, I, p. 108.
20 *WP*, III, p. 72.   21 *Mem.*, IV, p. 103.

me. Perhaps none is more notable than his steadfast refusal to suppose that the occasional vicissitudes of his career were drawbacks. Of the forty-six years that he devoted to the stage he managed the fortunes of the Yorkshire circuit for thirty-seven, until, that is, his death in 1803. Those fortunes were, he said, a "perplexing business."[22] Late in life, when ill not only with gout but with a broken leg, he declared, understandably enough, that "the stage has now no charms for me."[23] How, then, in the face of personal misfortune, of houses thinly attended, of his best actors being swept away to London, did he react? It is perhaps best expressed in his own words. "I can be truly reconciled."[24] After a serious dispute with one of his actresses, "We parted in a rage, [but] I flew to my philosophy to sustain the shock,"[25] or, with equal rapidity, to his bottle of Madeira.

I HAVE PERHAPS deferred longer than was necessary the facts of Tate Wilkinson's life, of which may I here present a brief résumé. He was born in London in 1739, and he was well born. His mother was the daughter of Alderman William Tate of Carlisle, of which city he was also on several occasions the mayor. Her family was connected with and friends of several persons of distinction and rank—Lord Forbes, Jonas Hanway, the Delavals of Seaton Delaval, Lord Galway—and so was that of his father, John Wilkinson, for some thirty years the minister of the Savoy Chapel in London. In 1752 an act of Parliament, the so-called Marriage Act, became law. The Chapel being extra-parochial, Tate's father believed that he had the right to issue licenses on his own authority. But in doing so he violated the provisions of the Act. In 1756 he was summoned for

[22] *Mem.*, II, p. 247.   [23] *Mem.*, II, p. 229.
[24] *WP*, I, p. 248.   [25] *WP*, III, p. 95.

trial, and sentenced to transportation for fourteen years. The convict ship set forth the following year, but Wilkinson died of gout while still on board, and was buried at Plymouth in Devonshire.

I have spoken of his son's addiction in later years to the consoling effects of Madeira. But at this very time he was already drinking a wine far more heady. He saw his first play when he was eight years old, and instantaneously entered into, as he wrote, "elysium."[26] And in this elysium, with the toy theatre he put together, he became overnight a manager. So solidly was he entrenched in this career that when in 1752 he was sent to Harrow at the age of thirteen he was aghast. In his *Memoirs* he records his feelings on this woeful occasion. "For a Manager to be sent to school was a stroke of real grief and horror."[27] But Harrow treated him well, and there, in an amateur production of a play by Cibber, he made his first appearance on the stage, trembling with nervousness.

Whenever he could he haunted the theatres of London, even more backstage than in the front of the house. He was alert and personable. His close friend, the eminent actress Mrs. Bellamy, said that he "was tall, his countenance rather sportive than beautiful, and his manners agreeable."[28] And in the eyes of all the professional performers he came to know, and to know well, he was unmistakably someone to whom the theatre was his only light, his only life.

He had already discovered his gift, a natural one which he improved and developed by incessant practice, for mimicry. It was this gift that first brought him fame, and a fame most deservedly won. Tate Wilkinson was possibly the greatest mimic who ever lived. His secret, he states, was that of feeling himself to be the person he imitated, and of

[26] *Mem.*, I, p. 21.   [27] *Mem.*, I, p. 39.
[28] *Mem.*, III, p. 187.

never exaggerating his words and actions into buffoonery.[29] This meant that he could assume not only the tone of voice of that person, but also his gait, manner, and even the expression of his face. Perhaps the most extraordinary element in this extraordinary skill of his was his ability to mimic in all these respects a woman. When he imitated the handsome actress Mrs. Woffington his face, to everybody's astonishment, became her face.[30] The timbre of his voice was naturally deep, but Bernard records as well a quality of sweetness in it that made the duplication of a woman's voice wholly effortless.[31]

By the time he was eighteen he knew and was known to a large segment of the theatrical world of London. On 18 April 1757 he was induced by his close friend, the great low comedian Edward Shuter, to try his luck as an actor. From that date to his final appearance on the stage, on 10 February 1801 at Leeds, he was almost without interruption before an audience.

He acted in all the principal theatres of the British Isles, at first gaining his greatest celebrity by means of his mimicry. The persons he mimicked were invariably other performers. He would, to the most enthusiastic applause, deliver a well-known speech of some eight or ten lines, giving in each separate line the manner and appearance of a different actor. He knew his ability, and he made full use of it, because as an actor, though well enough liked, he was never at any time considered more than second rate. When in 1800 a young actor made his first appearance in Yorkshire, Wilkinson was much pleased with his performance and, tapping him on the shoulder, remarked, "There's some

[29] *Mem.*, I, p. 54.
[30] Michael Kelly, *Reminiscences*, 2 vols. (London, 1826), II, p. 12.
[31] Bernard, *Retrospections*, I, p. 173, n. 8.

roast beef in you, Mr Wrench."[32] Of this particular nourishment Tate had been denied all but short rations.

His peregrinations brought him first to York for a brief visit in April 1763. He appeared there again as an actor, but not as an imitator, in 1764 and in 1765, from which period he made it his home and from 1770, as I have already mentioned, his kingdom. It is perhaps to be regretted that, except in private, he abandoned all efforts as a mimic from this time onward. Although a great many of the leading players of London appeared in York, usually for brief visits, they were not sufficiently well known to Yorkshire audiences. Imitations of their manner would therefore be without effect, and as manager it was obviously impolitic for him to mimic the members of his own company.

But, in fact, he did mimic them. When an actor did something to Wilkinson's dissatisfaction the unlucky man was obliged to watch all his mistakes being flawlessly reproduced. At the same time Tate could not allow this problem to be handled in only a negative and, as he probably thought, unkind fashion. The next morning the offending actor would receive a long letter in which he was advised constructively how to speak, to move, to behave.[33]

Wilkinson's skills as an impersonator and as a teacher were acknowledged by everybody. If as an actor he was far less successful he was at least never greeted with derision.[34] And, especially in his early years, his audiences must have applauded his diligence. In the calendar year 1770 we find him undertaking forty-one different parts, all leading ones: in Shakespeare Richard III, King John, Macbeth, Lear, Falstaff, Wolsey, Shylock, Richard II, Henry V, Othello,

[32] George Raymond, *The Life and Enterprises of Robert William Elliston* (London, 1857), p. 14.
[33] *Ibid.* [34] *WP*, I, pp. 197-198.

and Hamlet. These were chiefly tragedies. As a comedian he seems, particularly in plays written by Samuel Foote, to have had considerable success. He acted in high comedy, in farce, in comic opera. Toward the end of his life ill health curtailed these activities, and he did confess that "no boy was ever so weary of his tutor, or old maid of being chaste, as I am with thirty-four years rolling about in a restless theatrical hemisphere."[35] After 1801 he was not seen on the stage at all. In August 1803 he died quietly.[36] To his profession he had been a loyal servant, and to his company of players it was as though each individual member of it had lost, as Tate had lost in Joseph Baker, his own father.

THROUGHOUT THE entire length of his life Tate Wilkinson radiated, both as a man and as a manager, what I can only describe as innocence. It was the innocence of a man who knew no envy. It was the kindness of a manager who, whenever a new player came to York, would be the first to greet and to welcome him at the stagecoach or at the inn. It was the generosity that prompted him, even if that very player was unable to complete his engagement, to reimburse him with his full, i.e., prearranged, salary.[37] In saying this I do not mean an unworldly or unbusinesslike innocence, but rather that of honesty and of a simple, straightforward respect for the integrity of his profession.

In his two books one finds constant evidence of this quality. These books are a complete account of his life until 1795, when the second was published as *The Wandering Patentee; or, A History of the Yorkshire Theatres, from*

35 *Mem.*, IV, p. 69.

36 He was succeeded in the management by his eldest son, John Joseph Tate, who continued in that capacity until July 1814.

37 Bernard, *Retrospections*, I, pp. 179-180, n. 8.

1770 to the Present Time. The first, which appeared in 1790, is *Memoirs of His Own Life.* And never did two books reveal so entertainingly or so thoroughly what their author calls his "incoherent and fantastical disposition."[38] In them one searches in vain for any trace of a Simon Legree. But one does discover a man who had no illusions about himself. And, since that self was a manager's self, he had no illusions about the art of management.

"My calf volumes in my book-case, marked with *glaring golden* letters, WILKINSON'S WORKS, closely wedged and pent secure from moth and rust, the invincible Shakespear on one side, and Dryden on the other, as centinels of protection."[39] He says that he laughed out loud every time he looked at the bindings. But he knew too the value of what was inside them, and he was right. His books are very important contributions to the history of the English stage.

Now I am obliged to report that "WILKINSON'S WORKS" have not in the past been treated with any great degree of lenity on the part of many critics and historians. This is because of his helpless addiction to a garrulity of which he is most cheerfully aware. "I will be as various, prolix and tiresome, now and then, as the wind or the weather."[40] Even more pronounced than his prolixity is his love of digression. He describes his appearances in the summer of 1760 with a company playing at Winchester. On one occasion the audience was refractory and impolite. Aroused by this recollection, he pours out his reproof of unruly audiences in general for the next twenty-one pages.[41] Or again, in speaking of a visit to the London manager John Rich, he unluckily chances to mention that Mrs. Rich was a member of the Methodist Church. Up comes another of his favorite

[38] *WP*, I, p. viii.   [39] *WP*, I, p. 70.
[40] *WP*, I, p. 24.   [41] *Mem.*, II, pp. 239-260.

topics: twelve pages of resentment at Methodist preachers who inveigh against the sinfulness of everything connected with the stage.[42]

And yet one finds in this very failing an instance of his innocent and friendly honesty. After a long interruption of his narrative he will say, "Digression is so natural,"[43] or "But where was I?—Oh! I had just left Mr. Suett on the shelf at Hull,"[44] or "Says Tate Wilkinson, 'Don't pity me, reader, but pity my printer!' "[45] When he remarks that "the wild incoherent manner of my book is exactly my mode of conversation,"[46] I am altogether inclined to believe him.

He does write as if he were speaking. He does not labor for a fine flourish or a studied cadence. Like the best of us he is, of course, sometimes dull. But what above all else he achieved is the reader's impression that he is talking to somebody who is indeed both verbose and eccentric (that "infernal exotic," as Garrick called him,[47] or as he was dubbed by a friend at Hull, "one of God Almighty's Unaccountables"[48]), yet one whose word can be trusted.

For this trust he anxiously sought. He speaks of his constant desire to be accurate as to places and dates,[49] and until his day no historian of the stage had ever equalled him in bringing forward so many of them and, all in all, so correctly. He outlines his career without affectation and without vanity. Nor can there be any disagreement when we find him saying, "My books and bills from 1766 . . . in spite of my own inevitable blundering, will give me some

---

[42] *Mem.*, III, pp. 3-15.

[43] *Mem.*, III, p. 189.

[44] *WP*, I, p. 118.

[45] *WP*, I, p. 90.

[46] *WP*, I, p. 197. See, for examples of his manner of talking, Kelly, *Reminiscences*, II, pp. 10-11, n. 30; Mathews, *Memoirs*, I, pp. 391-394, n. 6; Samuel William Ryley, *The Itinerant* (London, 1817), III, pp. 115-116.

[47] *Mem.*, III, p. 45.

[48] *WP*, II, p. 266.

[49] *Mem.*, III, p. 58.

title for my being honoured with a place in a theatrical study."[50]

BUT HONOR CAME to him, too, in his lifetime. I have already referred to the attitude of the members of his company in thinking of him as if he were their father. Perhaps one cannot quite assume this to have been the case when, at the age of thirty-one, he first became a full-fledged manager. As time went by, however, no thoughtful actor could fail to understand that Tate's own understanding steadiness of purpose was to be preferred to harshness. Of course he had his troubles. Has any manager ever lived who has not had to contend with jealous actresses, with rebellious audiences, with players who must be dissuaded from assuming characters not suited to them?

From an anonymous pamphlet dealing with his theatre, published in 1788 and entitled *The Theatrical Register*, we glean a few details. His actors were sometimes visible to the audience as they stood in the wings. His scene men would shift the flats from an interior to an exterior after the scene was under way. His players more than once were guilty of that perennial complaint levelled at so many eighteenth-century actors: they had not memorized their lines.

He could and did respond. He could be firm, indeed stubborn. He insisted on constant all-around training—enunciation, deportment, dancing, fencing. He begged his

[50] *WP*, I, p. 15. I have not succeeded in tracing anything else written by Wilkinson except for his contributions to the theatrical periodical, *The Monthly Mirror*. These are footnotes to a series of articles entitled "History of the Stage," VII (March, June 1799), pp. 180, 357-358, 375. Also a letter to the editor, IX (April 1800), p. 233, referring to an episode described in *WP*, I, pp. 193-196. Also "Original Anecdotes respecting the Stage, and the Actors of the Old School, with Remarks on Mr. [Arthur] Murphy's 'Life of Garrick,' " XII (October, November 1801), pp. 267-271, 330-334; XIII (January, February 1802), pp. 43-48, 122-124; XIV (November 1802), pp. 335-337.

players to stay sober, because if, he remarks, they are "beholden to the assistance of the grape" they cannot be "good timeists on the stage."[51] He reprobated performers who did not, when acting, use handkerchiefs for blowing their noses and added, "How Adam and Eve managed such necessary business I cannot tell, but should be glad of information."[52] After hearing a comparable remark, I think it likely that the offending actor would laughingly agree to behave. Again, he speaks in forthright terms of one of the most notable bugbears, or perhaps dilemmas, of the acting profession. Parts, he insisted, do not make the actor; it is the actor who makes the part.

His company's dignity and well-being always remained his chief concern. When he became manager of the Yorkshire circuit his first reform was to abolish the degrading custom of an actor or actress pacing the streets, stopping passers-by and imploring them to take a ticket for his or her benefit night. He also insisted that on that night the actor should refrain from publicly thanking all those persons who had, in this fashion or in any other, helped to fill his pocketbook.

He would beg his company to dress appropriately. In his theatre, as in all others of his day, even in London, there was no general supervision as to this matter. Each actor, unless he had his private collection of stage dresses, would go to the theatre's wardrobe and choose from it whatever he thought was most suitable. But, do what he could, Wilkinson was obliged to confess that "strict propriety of habiliment not any manager has yet arrived at, even in London."[53] The women were far more at fault than the men, because love of finery might result in a chambermaid's stepping forth in a dress far more elegant than that of her mistress.

[51] *Mem.*, III, p. 241.　　[52] *WP*, II, p. 79.　　[53] *Mem.*, IV, p. 90.

An amusing paradox exists here. Tate's own fascination with gilt and spangles and velvet and ruffles was unconquerable. He would order from London costumes of the most extravagant opulence, hang them on a clothesline in his drawing room, and keep them there for days, while he gloated over them and made everybody else gloat too. A human weakness it was, which for once overcame his scruples as a manager. He would, in short, demand that these splendid dresses should sooner or later, and without being in any way altered, be made use of on the stage, and heroes would strut about in coats three sizes too large for them, and heroines in Indian war paint.[54]

Wilkinson's repertory of plays was the same as that of all English-speaking theatres throughout the entire eighteenth century, consisting of stock pieces: Shakespeare, Dryden, Cibber, Farquhar, and many others, and the new pieces that achieved success in the big London theatres. The number of eighteenth-century plays first acted anywhere else that attracted any attention is almost nonexistent. There is, in fact, only one that could be said to have survived: the Reverend John Home's tragedy entitled *Douglas*, first performed at Edinburgh in 1756, and thereafter acted all over the British Isles for the next hundred years at least. Wilkinson did bring forward a handful of new plays, written usually by members of his company, but they disappeared forever after two or three nights. Otherwise he was obliged to look to London.

I have referred earlier to Wilkinson's occasional problem in keeping his company just barely afloat. In the calendar year 1781 his receipts were £5,454 and his expenditures £5,031. But then, as he sorrowfully records, Garrick was the only manager who ever made any money.[55] His own

---

[54] Mathews, *Memoirs*, I, pp. 381-389, n. 6.
[55] *Mem.*, IV, p. 107.

salary was £1.11s.6d. a week, out of a total of £40 a week for his entire company.[56] His records reveal that he paid a certain young, untried actress exactly the same amount. She worked, may I add, with Tate for three laborious years, and when he released her to the Drury Lane manager in 1785 she was already the greatest comic actress of her day, in later years the idol of the English stage, the famous Mrs. Jordan. Another neophyte performer was at the same time being given a yet smaller salary, £1.5s. a week. By 1800, also at Drury Lane, this same actor was earning £31.10s. a week; his name was John Philip Kemble. Tate lined his own pockets to the extent that the probate of his will revealed his "Goods chattels and Credits" as amounting to less than £2,000.[57]

In operating his theatres he was orderly and efficient. "In my circuit," he says, "we never lose time; scenery, etc. being all ready at each theatre, unless for new pieces."[58] Everything moved with dispatch. A note on the York playbill for the last night of the 1785 season states that the farce, because of an actress's illness, had to be changed "to Rosina, And difficult to get that Perform'd, as all the Wardrobe is Pack'd and Loaded on the Waggons for Leeds." He would not allow his actors to make other commitments rashly. When in 1780 Sheridan wanted to procure Charles Lamb's later favorite, Richard Suett, for Drury Lane, Tate told Suett, highly popular and successful at York, of the risks

---

[56] Playbill, Sheffield, 14 October 1782, in Minster Library, York.

[57] His will, dated 14 November 1800, now in The Borthwick Institute of Historical Research, St. Anthony's Hall, York.

[58] *WP*, II, p. 131. The circuit maintained the same general schedule throughout all of Wilkinson's career. The dates, with the location of the theatre in each town, were as follows: York (Blake Street), February-May; Leeds (Hunslet Lane), June-July; York, August race week; Pontefract (Gillygate), August-September; Wakefield (Westgate), September; Doncaster (Magdalens), October; Hull (Finkle Street), October-January.

and uncertainties of acting in London, and before he let him go made Sheridan swear to give him a positive three-year engagement with an increase in salary every season.[59]

Whenever Suett or any other actor or actress spoke of Tate Wilkinson the word that rose instinctively to their lips was "generosity." A letter written from York to the actor Charles Mathews provides an admirable example. In August 1803 the comedian John Fawcett—in his early days long a member of the Yorkshire company—had come from London for a summer engagement with Wilkinson. He opened at Pontefract and made the stipulation that should the receipts not cover the expenses he was to receive no salary. This proved to be the case, and Fawcett stood by his word. At this juncture Wilkinson was seriously ill; he was, in fact, dying. But when he was given the news that, regardless of any promise, no money had changed hands, he became furiously angry and forced the theatre's treasurer to advance to Fawcett £25. The writer of the letter in question,[60] an actor in the York company, stated his belief that Wilkinson's distress and rage at what he considered an ungenerous state of affairs hastened his death, which took place in the afternoon of the following day.

Again, at the time of an actor's benefit Wilkinson made sure that he would always receive at least some return, no matter how small. Everything after the first £5 was invariably shared between actor and manager.[61] And at the conclusion of a somewhat more successful season than usual every performer was always given, in addition to his salary, a present "With the manager's kind compliments."[62]

As a man Tate Wilkinson was an unaccountable eccentric, but was blessed with a temperament that faced both pleas-

59 *WP*, II, pp. 98-99.
60 Mathews, *Memoirs*, I, pp. 411-412, n. 6.
61 *Ibid.*, I, p. 238n. 62 *Ibid.*, I, p. 401.

ure and toil with cheerfulness (I have also called it innocence). As a manager he was not only resilient but firm in his belief that genuine theatre was as beneficial as it was essential. These attributes are combined and illuminated perfectly in the concluding words of his last book.[63]

It is related of the Duke of Clarence, in the reign of Edward IV, that he chose to make his exit in a hogshead of Madeira; and as parting is a melancholy theme, I will instantly, in my present stupor, arouse my faculties with a bumper of the said liquor, as a health to all my *friends*, and the public at large —— *'Tis done!* —— it has gone down with a zest! —— O, I am comforted! —— And now with gratitude, and respectful regard, for all indulgences and errors, with every good will and wish for my brethren, praying for the success of theatres and universal patronage, with improving sense and wit on the stage, and good humour and lenity, with proper correction to keep the actors from being allowed to disgrace themselves, by never forgetting where they are, and the characters they represent, I remain to all and every one,

their most devoted, faithful,
honoured, and much obliged
humble servant,
TATE WILKINSON,
"Who adds to blockheads past one blockhead more."

[63] *WP*, IV, pp. 232-233.

"King Stephen" of the Park
and Drury Lane

BARNARD HEWITT

WASHINGTON IRVING customarily referred to Stephen Price as "King Stephen,"[1] and there was more than a touch of mockery in his figurative elevation of the American theatre manager to a throne. In the early nineteenth century, the struggle for independence from England was too recent for kings to be greatly admired in this country. They were associated not only with prestige and power but with arbitrariness and tyranny. When Irving called Price King Stephen, he was gently deriding the manager's manners and methods, as well as paying tribute to his prestige and power in the world of the theatre.

Stephen Price's parentage and the circumstances of his infancy did much to shape the King Stephen whom Washington Irving knew. Price was born in New York, the city on whose theatrical entertainment he was to put his stamp, on 25 September 1782, less than a year after Cornwallis' surrender at Yorktown and before peace with England had been formally ratified. He was the first son of Michael Price and Helena Cornwell.[2]

Little is known of his mother, but Michael Price had owned a farm in Red Bank, New Jersey, before the Revolution. In 1776 he sided with the Loyalists, moved to New York after the British occupied that city, and was a merchant there until shortly before the evacuation, when,

[1] Letter to Henry Brevoort, 15 March 1816, *The Letters of Washington Irving to Henry Brevoort*, 1 (New York, 1915).

[2] MS Notes on Trinity Churchyard Families, New York Historical Society.

like many others, he was indicted in August 1783 "for adhering to the enemies of the people" of the State of New York and fled, probably by ship, with his wife and infant son to Shelburne, Nova Scotia.[3] Unlike many who had chosen the losing side in the Revolutionary War, Michael Price did not remain in Nova Scotia. He returned to New York, probably early in 1784. Nothing has come to light regarding the conditions under which the Prices lived during this brief exile, but it is possible that in them lay the cause of the gout or arthritis from which Stephen suffered most of his adult life.

It speaks well for Michael's shrewdness and adaptability that he was able to resume business in New York, first as the operator of a boarding house, and then as a merchant.[4] He must somehow have managed to retain property he had acquired under the British occupation, and he eventually received some compensation from the British government for his farm in Red Bank, which had been confiscated by the State of New Jersey.[5]

Michael prospered. He had one daughter and three more sons, William, Edward, and Benjamin, who survived.[6] He was able to send Stephen, William, and Edward to Columbia College, and to set Benjamin up as a grocer.

Stephen graduated from Columbia in the class of 1799.[7] Alexander Hamilton's eldest son, Philip, graduated in the class of 1800. Stephen was almost surely the Price who was said to have accompanied Philip Hamilton when that un-

[3] MS American Loyalist Transcripts, xv, copy, New York Public Library.

[4] MS Loyalists, NYHS.

[5] MS American Loyalist Transcripts, xi.

[6] MS Notes on Trinity Churchyard Families; Michael Price Will, Wills, LVII, pp. 57-59, Hall of Records, New York City.

[7] *Catalogue of the Officers and Graduates of Columbia College in the City of New York, 1754-1888* (New York, 1888).

fortunate young man was killed in a duel with a politician named George L. Eaker, 3 November 1801. An account of this duel provides a first tenuous connection between Stephen Price and the world of the theatre: Eaker's second was Thomas A. Cooper, leading actor of the Old American Company at the Park, then called the New Theatre.[8]

After graduating from Columbia, Stephen must have read law in the office of some established lawyer, which was then the only way to prepare for the legal profession, for on 18 February 1804 he received a license, signed by DeWitt Clinton, Mayor of New York City, to appear as attorney-at-law in the Mayor's Court.[9] For four or five years, he practiced mostly criminal law, according to Mordecai Noah,[10] perhaps entirely in the Mayor's Court, for I have found no evidence that he was licensed to practice elsewhere.

He must have spent a good deal of time at the Park Theatre, however, and gained the friendship of Thomas Cooper, who became its lessee and manager in 1806, for in the summer of 1808 Price bought a share in the Park management. The only public notice of this was the announcement by "The Managers"—plural—that the new season would begin on 9 September.[11]

The theatre with which Price was to be so long associated had been modeled after eighteenth-century English theatres and built facing City Hall Park in 1798. Financed by shares sold to New York citizens, it cost $130,000, more than three times the amount anticipated. For a variety of reasons its managers had not prospered, and in April 1806 John Jacob Astor and John Beekman had bought the building from the

[8] Charles H. Winfield, *History of Hudson County, New Jersey* (New York, 1899), pp. 203-205.

[9] MS Licenses, Museum of the City of New York.

[10] Letter to the Editor, *Dramatic Mirror* (New York), 8 February 1840.

[11] *American Citizen*, New York, 31 August 1808.

shareholders for $50,000 and leased it to Cooper at a rental of $8,400 a year, payable in quarterly installments, making available to him a maximum of $20,000 for improvements.[12]

When Price bought into the management in 1808, the Park probably held 2,372: 1,272 in three tiers of boxes, 500 in the pit, and 600 in the gallery.[13] At prices of $1, 50¢, and 25¢, it could produce about $1,600 when full.

In spite of the original cost and the improvements made when Cooper became lessee, the exterior decoration had never been completed; the cupola and the pediment remained empty of the sculpture they had been designed to hold. The exterior was not only unfinished; it was ill-kept. An observer in the fall of 1809 remarked on "the barbarous front . . . resembling a miserable barrack, stretching its crazy shoulders over a brick wall, here and there interspersed with a few broken panes of glass," and asked, "Is this . . . the *grand* front of the *new* theatre of New-York? Do these bare joists and filthy walls bespeak wealthy proprietors? Do these streams of *indescribable* distillation, which run from its sides along the pavement, indicate the cleanliness or delicacy of the managers?"[14] The $20,000 must have been spent inside, for the same observer pronounced the interior "in point of decoration . . . very little inferior to the handsomest theatres of France, Italy, and England."[15]

The horseshoe-shaped auditorium was lighted by patent oil lamps; in 1809 these were replaced by a large chandelier with candles, suspended from the center of the domed ceil-

---

[12] Liber Conveyances, LXXII, p. 514, Hall of Records, New York; *Evening Post* (New York), 22 April 1806.

[13] G.C.D. Odell, *Annals of the New York Stage*, II (New York, 1927), p. 291.

[14] *Rambler's Magazine and New York Theatrical Register*, I (September-December 1809), pp. 10, 110.

[15] *Rambler's Magazine*, I, p. 14.

ing, a smaller one on either side of the proscenium, and still smaller ones "dispersed around the second and third tiers of boxes."[16] Dimensions of the stage are not available, but it projected 12 to 15 feet into the auditorium to form a wide apron flanked on either side by a proscenium door and stage boxes. The stage was lighted by oil lamps or by candles in the form of footlights at the front of the apron and of wing lights attached to the wing flats on either side behind the proscenium arch.

The company of actors was generally regarded as inferior to that at the Chestnut Street Theatre in Philadelphia. It was without distinction except for its manager, Thomas Cooper, then thirty-two years old and the best leading actor on the American stage in both tragedy and comedy. He was unusually versatile, playing Charles Surface and Hamlet, Romeo and Shylock, Hotspur and Othello.

In the fall of 1808 the Park Company presented stock plays of the late eighteenth-century repertory three or four nights a week, with a nightly change of bill. Cooper appeared in all of his principal roles until December, when he left for starring engagements in Philadelphia and Boston. Because of "the unfavorable state of the weather" and poor business, the theatre was closed from 5 January to 22 February. The economy was suffering from the Embargo Act of 1807, which cut off trade with Europe.

In February the management presented the American-born actor John Howard Payne. He was billed as Master Payne in imitation of the child prodigy Master Betty, who at the age of thirteen in leading adult roles had been sensationally successful in 1804-05 on the English stage. Payne was hardly a child—he was nearly eighteen—but he was handsome and a protégé of some prominent New Yorkers. He attracted nearly full houses for his debut and for his

16 *Rambler's Magazine*, I, p. 18.

benefit. In the six performances between, he did well enough to be re-engaged in May, when he averaged $500 a night, exclusive of his benefit.[17] The other success of the season was *The Forty Thieves*, a romantic musical spectacle new to New York.

The 1809-10 season was similar to the preceding one. The stock company played to poor houses in the fall. Before the winter closing, only *The Africans*, a new and spectacular melodrama by George Colman the younger, drew well. Two more melodramas, James Kenney's *Ella Rosenberg* and Frederic Reynolds' *The Exile*, plus starring engagements by Payne and by John Dwyer from England, a handsome and elegant portrayer of young men in standard comedy, bolstered receipts somewhat in the spring.

It must have been obvious to Cooper and Price that the stock company alone could not regularly attract adequate audiences. What the public wanted was visiting stars like Payne and Dwyer or spectacles like *The Forty Thieves* and *The Africans*. Spectacles were costly to produce and took time to prepare. Two or three a season were about all that could be got up under the repertory system. Stars added to the expense but not so much as spectacles did, and they appeared in standard plays, which could be staged with stock scenery and costumes. Therefore, when Cooper sailed for England in June of 1809, although he went seeking recruits to strengthen the stock company, he was looking particularly for stars.

He was surprisingly successful. Exercising remarkable enterprise, resourcefulness, and persistence, he persuaded George Frederick Cooke, the great though undependable tragic actor of Covent Garden Theatre, to perform in America, and in spite of Cooke's vacillation and drunken caprices

17 William Dunlap, *A History of the American Theatre* (New York, 1832), p. 350.

—he was an alcoholic—managed to get him on a ship bound for New York. Cooper engaged Cooke to play in New York, Boston, Philadelphia, and Baltimore for ten months at twenty-five guineas a week, a clear benefit in each city, passage across the Atlantic, and twenty-five cents a mile for traveling expenses in America.[18] Exclusive of the benefits and travel expenses, this amounted to $14,000, or about $120 a night.[19]

News of Cooke's coming created a sensation. When he opened on 21 November 1810, the audience crowded every corner of the Park Theatre. Receipts were $1820, and would have been more if in the crush some had not got in without paying. The seventeen nights of Cooke's first New York engagement grossed $21,578.[20] The managers paid Cooke $1920 for sixteen performances plus $1878, the gross receipts of his benefit. Nightly expenses were probably no more than $300. Price and Cooper must have made well over $12,000.

Cooke then played engagements in Boston, Philadelphia, and Baltimore, interspersed with return engagements in New York. The terms of his engagement in Philadelphia are specified in William Warren's diary.[21] For each of Cooke's first five performances there Price and Cooper received one-half the receipts after expenses of $300 a night, for his sixth performance all the receipts after $300, for his next six performances as for the first six, and for his thirteenth performance the gross receipts. Warren paid Price and Cooper $8809.16 for the twenty nights of Cooke's two engagements. Out of this they presumably paid Cooke $2280 for nineteen performances, $1356.16 the receipts of his clear benefit, and

18 William Dunlap, *Memoirs of George Fred. Cooke, Esq.*, 2 vols. (London, 1813), II, pp. 112-145.

19 *Columbian* (New York), 19 November 1810.

20 Dunlap, *Memoirs of Cooke*, II, pp. 156, 158, 174.

21 30 April 1811, MS, Channing Pollock Collection, Howard University.

about $90 for travel—a total of $3735. Their profit was about $5000. We may assume similar arrangements in Baltimore and Boston. Although Cooke's drawing power declined the longer he performed, because of drink and disease, he was highly profitable to Price and Cooper.

From the moment of Cooke's arrival in New York, Price took a great deal of trouble about his valuable property. He saw Cooke through customs, entertained for him, protected him from unwanted attention, accompanied him to Boston by boat and stage, commissioned his portrait by Gilbert Stuart, and sent William Dunlap to look after him in Philadelphia. He even took Cooke into his house as a permanent guest, until Cooke found that this arrangement interfered with his drinking.[22]

Tension with Great Britain over that country's interference with American shipping, which had been growing since 1806, culminated in Congress's declaration of war on 18 June 1812. The war prevented Price and Cooper from duplicating the success they had had with Cooke. They announced that they "had nearly conclude an arrangement" with John Philip Kemble, then London's leading tragic actor, which the hostilities had "necessarily suspended."[23]

The war did not entirely preclude movement between the belligerent countries. In July 1812, Joseph George Holman and his daughter, of the London stage, managed somehow to get out of England and to make their debuts at the Park Theatre in September. Miss Holman proved moderately attractive in elegant comedy, but her father was too old and ill to contribute much to the Park. They were no adequate substitutes for John Kemble or for Cooke, who died on 12 September.

[22] Dunlap, *Memoirs of Cooke*, II, pp. 154, 163, 174, 184, 190.
[23] *Columbian* (New York), 31 August 1812.

Business was so bad that season and the next that in September 1814 Price informed Astor that unless the rent was reduced he and Cooper would have to give up their lease. Astor refused, but they did not relinquish the theatre.[24]

The war formally ended 24 December 1814, with the signing of the Treaty of Ghent, but because of the slowness of communication, fighting continued into the following March. In the summer of 1815, Cooper sold his share in the Park management to Price, in order to devote himself wholly to starring engagements.

Early in the fall, Price made his first trip to England in search of plays and players, leaving the Park in charge of Edmund Simpson, a mainstay of the stock company since 1809 and stage manager since 1812.[25] Price made generous offers to Eliza O'Neill, who was regarded as a likely successor to Mrs. Siddons, and to Charles Incledon, the popular singing actor, but both were committed elsewhere.[26] He returned early in April with no stars but with several useful additions to the stock company and with John Howard Payne's new play *The Accusation, or, The Family Anglade,* fresh from Drury Lane, where it had had its premiere on 1 February.[27]

In May of 1816 occurred the first episode in a real-life drama, on which rested to a considerable extent Price's reputation for being an implacable enemy. J. G. Millingen, quoting "from American newspapers," describes the events

24 Kenneth Wiggins Porter, *John Jacob Astor, Business Man,* 2 vols. (Cambridge, Mass., 1931), II, p. 990.

25 Odell, *Annals,* II, p. 387.

26 Washington Irving letter to Brevoort, 15 March 1816; *Courier,* London, 22 February 1816.

27 Odell, *Annals,* II, pp. 453ff.; Grace Overmyer, *America's First Hamlet: John Howard Payne* (New York, 1957), p. 397, n. 71.

leading up to one of two duels which Price presumably fought.[28] I say "presumably," because duelling was a capital crime, and a search of newspapers now available failed to reveal Millingen's source. All I found was a notice that the funeral of Benjamin Price, Stephen's youngest brother, would be held on 13 May 1816 from the residence of Stephen Price, 352 Broadway.[29]

According to the account in Millingen, one night when Benjamin was at the Park Theatre with a beautiful young woman, a British officer named Green in the next box "took the liberty of turning round and staring her full in the face." She complained to Benjamin, and "on a repetition of the offence, he seized the officer's nose full between his finger and thumb, and wrung it effectively." After some words, both men apologized, and Green went off to join his regiment in Canada. Unfortunately, news of the episode followed him, and his brother officers, especially a Captain Wilson, insisted that he avenge the insult. Consequently, Green returned to New York and challenged Benjamin. "They fought at Hoboken, and Ben was killed in the first fire." Green crossed the river in a small boat, boarded a vessel in the bay, and escaped to England. Some time later (Millingen gives no date), Captain Wilson, on his way from Canada to England, stopped in New York and boasted publicly of his part in the killing of Benjamin. News of this reached Stephen, who was ill with gout. He rose from his bed, dressed, sought out Wilson at the Washington Hotel, and challenged him. They fought on Bedloe's Island "and Wilson fell dead at the first shot."

Price took Simpson into a quarter partnership in the season of 1816-17,[30] and the managers unsuccessfully

28 *The History of Duelling*, 2 vols. (London, 1841), I, pp. 381-385.
29 *Columbian* (New York), 13 May 1816.
30 *Blunt's Stranger's Guide to the City of New York* (New York,

attempted to increase the number of performances from three or four to six a week. They were able to present few stars and no new ones from across the Atlantic, unless we count the horses in James West's equestrian company. West had arrived unable to pay the passage for his horses and their riders. Price and Simpson advanced the necessary money, and the "horse and foot" began a successful engagement at the Park Theatre on 20 January 1817, in the spectacular melodrama *Timour the Tartar*.[31]

The 1817-18 season was bolstered considerably by delayed fruits of Price's trip to England. Charles Incledon, at sixty still one of the most popular singing actors on the English stage, made his debut at the Park on 20 October 1817, and he was followed almost immediately by Thomas Philipps, also a very popular English singer, younger, more engaging, and a better actor than Incledon. Incledon returned to the Park in February, and Philipps played several engagements there before returning to England in May of 1819, having profited by more than $37,000.[32] What had begun successfully with Cooke was now an established policy. Price presented each star first at the Park and brought him back for return engagements between bookings in other cities.

But Incledon and Philipps were not enough. In April 1818 Price sent Simpson to England for more performers. He had little immediate success. John Sinclair, Catherine Stephens, Eliza O'Neill, and Edmund Kean, the new star of Drury Lane, were all either engaged, too expensive, or un-

---

1817), p. 135; Joe Cowell, *Thirty Years Passed Among the Players in England and America* (New York, 1844), p. 50.

31 Cowell, *Thirty Years*, p. 64; Odell, *Annals*, ii, pp. 469-470.

32 Odell, *Annals*, iii, p. 305.

willing to go to America.[33] Not until a few years later, when more intrepid artists had returned with their pockets full of dollars, did the rush across the Atlantic begin.

Nevertheless, Simpson's efforts were not unfruitful. He signed Robert Maywood, tragedian from Drury Lane, for fourteen nights for one-third of the receipts after expenses and a clear benefit. He met James W. Wallack, in his early twenties, ambitious, and overshadowed by Kean at Drury Lane, and paved the way for Wallack's debut at the Park in September 1818. He did not sign Mr. and Mrs. Bartley, but they came on their own and made their debuts at the Park in November.[34] And he brought back several recruits for the stock company.

In the 1818-19 season, the managers again tried six performances a week, but New York suffered a business crisis late in 1818 and the added performance proved unprofitable. They no longer depended on the stock company in standard repertory to do more than fill in one or two nights between the departure of one star and the arrival of another. If no star was available for a period of several weeks, the stock company was presented in new plays, shows with spectacular scenery, or other novelties.

The 1819-20 season began well at the end of August with Wallack in a starring engagement, but yellow fever, which plagued the eastern seaboard each summer, was so bad that the Park was forced to close from 18 September to 6 October.[35] After it reopened, the Bartleys, Cooper, and Wallack starred in succession and in combination until the Park

[33] Philip H. Highfill, "Edmund Simpson's Talent Raid on England in 1818" (1), *Theatre Notebook*, XII (Spring, 1958), pp. 87-88.

[34] Highfill, "Edmund Simpson's Talent Raid" (2), *Theatre Notebook*, XII (Summer, 1958), pp. 133, 134, 135.

[35] Odell, *Annals*, II, p. 552.

closed from 4 January to 21 February because of bad
weather and bad business. Eighteen-nineteen was a year
of bank failures and bankruptcies.

It is probable that some time in the fall of 1819 Price
crossed the Atlantic again, although the only evidence for
this is a note in Dunlap's diary, 16 December 1819: "I learn
. . . that Price has large executions out against him and has
gone to England."[36] Price may have been evading more
than creditors. Scoville says, "It was about this time that
John Slidell [later United States Senator from Louisiana
and after the secession Confederate commissioner to
France] had a duel with Stephen Price, the manager of the
Park Theatre. They fought in the morning and Slidell shot
his antagonist, giving him a bad wound. It was the failure
of his firm, McKenzie and McCrea, Merchants [McKenzie
changed his name to Slidell when he left New York] that
determined him to go to a new state."[37] According to Sears,
Slidell went to New Orleans in 1819, but Sears mentions no
duel.[38] Beckles says that the duel was the cause of Slidell's
abrupt departure and that it was fought over an actress in
the Park Theatre company.[39]

Perhaps Price felt it would be safer to recuperate outside
New York, and in England he could scout for more stars.
If he went on this occasion, he surely negotiated with Ed-
mund Kean to come to America the following season.

In any case, he was in New York in March, for on the
eighteenth of that month he stood sponsor at the baptism

36 William Dunlap, *The Diary of William Dunlap*, 3 vols. (New
York, 1829-31), II, 500.

37 Joseph A. Scoville, *The Old Merchants of New York City*, 5 vols.
(New York, 1865), II, pp. 295ff.

38 Louis Martin Sears, *John Slidell* (Durham, N. C., 1925), p. 8.

39 Willson Beckles, *John Slidell and the Confederates in Paris, 1862-
65* (New York, 1932), pp. 10-11.

of Mary Elizabeth Seton in Trinity Church.[40] Thus he was on hand in good time to witness the final disaster of a calamitous season.

Early in the morning of 25 May, after a performance for the author's benefit of Mordecai Noah's new play *Yusef Caramalli; or The Siege of Tripoli,* a fire which started in the Park's carpenter shop quickly spread through the entire structure, and completely destroyed the building and its contents. Price and Simpson were insured for $12,000 but lost much more than that in scenery and costumes. Members of the company lost their entire wardrobes valued at upwards of $30,000.[41]

On the day of the fire, Price punctiliously sent Noah his portion of the receipts, amounting to $405.12. Noah generously returned the money for distribution among the members of the company.[42]

The managers moved energetically to make the best of their bad situation. Four days after the destruction of the Park the company resumed performances in the smaller, less comfortable theatre on Anthony Street, where it continued until 4 July.

Perhaps Price and Simpson saw in the disaster an opportunity to escape from landlords Astor and Beekman, for on 12 June 1820 Simpson petitioned the New York Common Council to lease a lot on Chambers Street as a site for a theatre at $1500 a year for forty-two years. On 10 July the petition was denied.[43] Astor and Beekman were slow to start rebuilding, and on 30 August Price and Simpson

---

[40] "Records of Baptism in Trinity Church," *New York Genealogical and Biographical Record,* LXXII (1941).

[41] *American* (New York), 25 May 1820; *Letters from John Pintard,* 4 vols. (New York, 1940), I, pp. 292, 293.

[42] *Columbian* (New York), 27 May 1820.

[43] Minutes of the New York Common Council, Hall of Records, New York City.

announced plans to build on another site a theatre somewhat smaller than the Park at a cost of $75,000, to be
financed by the sale of $500 shares to bear six percent
interest.[44] Nothing came of this. The question of whether
the managers were serious and failed to sell enough shares
or were merely trying to prod Astor and Beekman remains
unanswered.

While Price went off to England to escort Edmund Kean
to America, his company opened the 1820-21 season on
4 September at the Anthony Street Theatre. Two new plays
were successful in the interim before Kean's eagerly
awaited arrival. Sheridan Knowles's *Virginius*, which had
been acclaimed at Covent Garden the previous May,
opened on 25 September, and J. R. Planché's spectacular
The Vampire; or, The Bride of the Isles opened on 23 October, less than three months after its premiere at the English
Opera House.[45]

Price and Kean arrived in New York on 10 November,
and on 29 November Kean made his American debut as
Richard III to a packed house. As in England, critical
reactions differed regarding this little actor and his displays
of overpowering emotion, but people were eager to see him.
Receipts for his sixteen nights averaged nearly $1000. The
managers paid Kean $222 a night for fourteen nights; $698,
half the gross receipts of his first benefit; and about $500 for
his second benefit—a total of about $4300.[46] We can assume
nightly expenses of $300 and estimate that Price and Simp-
son profited by about $7000.

Evidence is lacking that Price and Simpson profited from

44 *National Advocate* (New York), 30 August 1820.

45 Odell, *Annals*, II, pp. 578, 579.

46 A.L.S., Edmund Simpson to Thomas Philipps, 7 December 1820;
Kean memorandum in J. Fitzgerald Molloy, *The Life and Adventures
of Edmund Kean 1787-1833*, 2 vols. (London, 1888), extra illustrated,
Widener Library, Harvard.

Kean's engagements in Philadelphia, Baltimore, and Boston as they had from Cooke's. Kean recorded the terms of his first Philadelphia engagement: for twelve nights, half the receipts after expenses; for two benefits, half the gross receipts.[47] He received $5747 for those sixteen performances.[48] For his second engagement in Boston, he contracted with Snelling Powell to perform four nights a week for two weeks, sharing receipts after $2000, and to receive the gross receipts for his benefit on the ninth night.[49] Even if the New York managers did not receive a commission on Kean's appearances elsewhere, they did very well out of his thirty-three performances at the Anthony Street Theatre.

Kean dominated the 1820-21 season at the Anthony Street Theatre. The first Joseph Jefferson, however, a popular comic actor and grandfather of the great Joe Jefferson, made his last appearance there in March, and Henry Wallack, James's older brother, made his American debut there in May. Payne's new melodrama *Thérèse; or The Orphan of Geneva*, fresh from Drury Lane, opened on 30 April and drew well through the remainder of the season, which ended on 4 July.

By that time Price was in London again. He had sailed for Liverpool on 11 May,[50] probably having waited only until he had signed a lease at $13,000 a year for the new Park which was under construction by Astor and Beekman.[51] While Price was en route to England, his father Michael died.[52] Michael's will, probated 27 October, reveals that he owned valuable real estate in land and buildings, and that Stephen came into a considerable property, even

[47] Kean memorandum.
[48] William Warren Diary, 13 February 1821, Howard University.
[49] Edmund Kean autograph letters, Folger Shakespeare Library.
[50] *Evening Post* (New York), 12 May 1821.
[51] Porter, *John Jacob Astor*, II, p. 990.
[52] *National Advertiser* (New York), 22 May 1821.

though he shared the estate with his mother, his sister, and his brothers William and Edward.[53]

In London, Price tried unsuccessfully to hire the singing actor John Braham. He engaged Thomas Philipps for a second American tour and several lesser lights. One of these was the comedian Joe Cowell, who has left a graphic description of the New York manager. Price invited Cowell to breakfast in his lodgings in Norfolk Street. There Cowell found Price lying on the bed clad in a "wadded silk dressing gown" with his feet wrapped in flannel. Price explained with considerable profanity that a late night in the company of James Wallack had brought on an attack of gout. He spoke with deliberation, Cowell says, "in a peculiarly distinct and drawling manner." He had "small, bright, mischievous eyes, an abominable nose—looking like a large thumb, very much swollen and nearly 'coming to a head,' " but a firm, decisive mouth. Altogether his was not a face that could be called "good," although it was "capable of an extremely agreeable expression." Cowell observed that Price looked fifty and talked like twenty; he was thirty-eight.

Cowell was acting at Astley's for the summer and engaged at the Adelphi for the fall, but he had publicly expressed support for Queen Caroline when she was accused of adultery, and he knew he would have no difficulty in securing a release. He eagerly accepted Price's offer of £10 a week for the first year and £12 for the second.[54]

Price sailed from Liverpool on 1 September bringing with him Thomas Philipps and large quantities of costumes for a spectacular production consisting of *Henry IV Part 2* and the coronation scene from *Henry V*, in imitation of

53 Wills, LVII, pp. 57-59, Hall of Records, New York City.
54 Cowell, *Thirty Years*, pp. 49-51.

those which had been presented at Drury Lane and Covent Garden in honor of the recent accession of George IV to the throne.[55] When Price reached New York, his company was already established in the new Park Theatre, which had been opened with suitable ceremony on 1 September.

The new theatre fronted 80 feet on City Hall Park and extended 135 feet in depth. It was 85 feet high to the top of the cornice. A substantial wing on Theatre Alley housed greenroom and dressing rooms. A ticket lobby 47 feet 6 inches long and 9 feet wide opened into the main lobby, which was 147 feet long. Doors from it gave access to the auditorium, which was lyre-shaped and seated 2500 in three full circles of boxes, two "side tiers," a commodious pit, and a capacious gallery.

The stage was 52 feet 6 inches wide at the stage boxes, 38 feet wide at the proscenium opening, 70 feet deep from the front of the apron, and 40 feet from floor to ceiling. In the proscenium on either side of the apron was a door. The auditorium was lighted by patent oil lamps in three chandeliers—one hanging from the dome of the auditorium ceiling and one on each side on brackets attached to the downstage proscenium columns above the first tier of boxes. Footlights and wing lights illuminated the stage.[56] The new Park Theatre was assessed at $80,000 in 1823.[57]

Newspaper descriptions praised the interior decoration, designed and executed by American artists, but Joe Cowell was not favorably impressed. He found the auditorium excessively dark, with only ten or twelve lamps in the large chandelier and half as many in each of the two smaller ones.

[55] *The Drama or Theatrical Magazine* (London), 1 (October 1821), p. 312.

[56] *Evening Post* and *National Advocate* (New York), 1 September 1821; James Hardie, *The Description of the City of New York* (New York, 1827), p. 341.

[57] Porter, *John Jacob Astor*, II, p. 990.

The managers had tried unsuccessfully to persuade Astor and Beekman to install gas. The decoration on the front of the boxes, "in the Grecian style," according to a newspaper description, Cowell said was "designed in the taste of an upholsterer, and executed without any taste at all."[58]

Philipps began his first engagement on 17 October. Cowell made his debut on 30 October and proved a popular addition to the stock company. Philipps returned in November for a second engagement, and he was followed by James Wallack just arrived from England. Thomas Cooper followed Wallack, and Philipps played a third engagement at the end of January. The spectacular *Henry IV Part 2*, with the costumes Price had brought from England, opened 4 February and proved very popular.[59] In the spring there were fewer stars and more novelties. Of the latter, the most successful were a dramatization of James Fenimore Cooper's new novel *The Spy* and a grand ballet, *La Belle Peruvienne*, featuring dancers Tatin and Labasse and quantities of spectacular scenery. Wallack was unable to return until May, when he played on crutches, for he had broken a leg when his coach overturned on the way to Philadelphia in December. Cooper played his second engagement in June.

Before Cooper's arrival, however, Price was off to England again on the same ship with Wallack.[60] In August rumors came back that Wallack would return in December, that John Braham had been engaged, and that the witty, eccentric comedian Charles Mathews would arrive on the next ship. Mathews did arrive the evening of 5 September, accompanied by Price.[61] Because New York was suffering

58 Cowell, *Thirty Years*, p. 57; *Evening Post* (New York), 1 September 1821.

59 Odell, *Annals*, III, p. 20.

60 J. W. Wallack memorandum book, Folger.

61 *Albion*, New York, 31 August and 7 September 1822.

an unusually severe outbreak of yellow fever, they did not stop in the city but proceeded to Thomas Cooper's home in Bristol, Pennsylvania.[62] Also because of the yellow fever, the company did not open the 1822-23 season until 9 September, and then not in the new theatre but in the open-air Circus on Broadway where it was thought that there would be less danger of contagion. Price sent Mathews to perform first in Baltimore and Philadelphia, where the yellow fever was not so prevalent as it was in New York.

Mathews was famous in England not so much for his acting in plays as in his "At Homes," one-man entertainments of his own devising in which he told anecdotes of contemporary life, delivered monologues, sang songs, and impersonated a number of varied and eccentric characters. On the voyage to America, Price handed Mathews a copy of *Monsieur Tonson*, William Moncrieff's popular farce, and suggested that he begin with Monsieur Morbleu in that play and other standard roles, saving his At Homes for later.[63] In Baltimore Price saw Mathews act Goldfinch in Thomas Holcroft's *The Road to Ruin* and Morbleu in *Monsieur Tonson*, and advised him strongly to perform those roles in his New York debut.[64]

The yellow fever subsided with the coming of cooler weather. The company returned to the Park on 4 November, and on 7 November Mathews made his New York debut, in accord with Price's advice, to a $1700 house. He played seven more performances in standard plays to excellent audiences. For his benefit on a rainy night he drew $1800, just about capacity. He shared the receipts after

[62] Mrs. Charles Mathews, *Memoirs of Charles Mathews, Comedian*, 4 vols. (London, 1839), III, pp. 301, 306.

[63] Mathews, *Memoirs*, III, p. 372.

[64] Mathews, *Memoirs*, III, p. 327.

expenses for seven performances and earned a total of $10,962 for eight nights' work.[65]

Mathews was immediately "re-engaged" and announced for a series of At Homes. The first of these, entitled *A Trip to Paris*, drew an $1800 house, but the auditorium proved too large and the audience too noisy for this intimate entertainment. For the second At Home, receipts dropped considerably. Thereafter, Mathews combined the material of his At Homes with performances in standard farces.[66]

Price not only advised Mathews shrewdly about his repertory, but generally looked after the comedian as carefully as he had looked after Cooke, although not for quite the same reasons. Mathews was frightened of yellow fever, quite justifiably. Moreover, he was intolerant of much that he found in America. Cowell says, "Price followed him like a shadow. . . . His uncontrolled expressions of disgust at everything American would have speedily ended his career, but that Price managed to have him continually surrounded by a certain set, who had good sense enough to admit his talent as ample amends for his rudeness."[67] In February Price accompanied Mathews to Philadelphia by sleigh and remained with him through his second engagement there. When Mathews returned to New York in April, he boarded in the same house with Price.[68]

Price advised Mathews to travel to Boston by sea, which the comedian found pleasant. In Boston he had apparently contracted to share the receipts after expenses, plus a benefit, of course, and he complained to Price that although he had drawn what Bostonians called good houses, the

65 Mathews, *Memoirs*, III, p. 331.   66 Odell, *Annals*, III, pp. 49-52.
67 Cowell, *Thirty Years*, p. 62.
68 Mathews, *Memoirs*, III, pp. 375, 405. Price must have been living in a boarding house; no residence is listed for him in *Longworth's New York Directory* after 1820.

average was only $750, which because of their "shameful charge" did not give him £50 ($222) a night. Price re-engaged him for four nights in February and guaranteed him his £50 a night. Because the winter weather discouraged theatregoing and Mathews' novelty had somewhat worn off, the Park management lost money.[69]

Beginning 3 April, Mathews played eighteen more performances at the Park, appearing in a number of new characters before his farewell on 19 May. On 17 May, he played *Othello*. He did not burlesque the role. Cowell says Price "cajoled" Mathews into this rash experiment.[70] Mrs. Mathews thought she remembered that Price had bet Mathews he couldn't do it.[71] Bad though tiny Mathews must have been as the Moor, the performance drew a full house. Price had scored again. Mathews' first American tour was immensely profitable to him, and he gave Price full credit for his success.

Mathews was not the only star of the Park's 1822-23 season. Cooper, James Wallack, Thomas Philipps, and Mrs. Gilfert, formerly Miss Holman, all played one or more engagements. Other special attractions included a mirror drop 33 feet by 17 feet 6 inches weighing nearly two tons, which was unveiled 19 February; the New York premiere of *Tom and Jerry; or Life in London*, the immensely popular burletta "of fun, frolic, fashion and flash" on 3 March; and from 14 March through 5 April a series of equestrian dramas.[72]

The equestrian dramas were intended to meet competition from the circuses which each year for part of the season drew audiences away from the Park. James West's company was especially attractive. Competition was

---

[69] Mathews, *Memoirs*, III, pp. 346, 372.
[70] Cowell, *Thirty Years*, p. 63.   [71] Mathews, *Memoirs*, III, p. 408.
[72] Odell, *Annals*, III, pp. 58-61.

beginning on other fronts. Summer seasons at Chatham Garden and at Mrs. Baldwin's little Warren Street Theatre tended to begin early and run into the fall. Moreover, Charles Gilfert, manager of the theatre in Charleston, South Carolina, was talking of building a theatre on the Bowery. Gilfert had lured the comedian Thomas Hilson away from the Park. The managers of the Park created the impression that they were about to expand into the circus business, that they were planning to build on Broadway a splendid amphitheatre like Astley's in London. As a result they were able to buy West out—lease, building, engagements, horses, and scenery—and to obtain from him an agreement not to establish another circus in the United States. Moreover, they persuaded Joe Cowell to manage the circus, allowing his place in the Park company to be filled once more by Thomas Hilson.[73]

In the 1823-24 season, the most glamorous importation was the singing actor William Pearman from the English Opera House, who made his debut at the Park on 5 November and returned in March and May. William Augustus Conway, a tall, handsome tragedian of the Kemble school, opened as Hamlet on 12 January and made a considerable success. Paired with Thomas Cooper in two later engagements, he drew good audiences. Novelties included a revival of *The Tempest* with special scenery; the American premiere of John Howard Payne's opera *Clari; or, The Maid of Milan*, with Pearman singing Jocoso, a role he had created in London; and a new comic pantomime, *Harlequin's Frolics*, featuring Schinotti, a pantomimist and dancer.[74]

The managers of the Park clearly depended on stars, preferably new ones from abroad, and on new pieces, preferably combining music and spectacular scenery. For the

[73] Cowell, *Thirty Years*, p. 64.   [74] Odell, *Annals*, III, pp. 93-107.

1824-25 season, they were able to secure only one new star of any brilliance, Lydia Kelly of Drury Lane, a charming comedienne who played two engagements in such roles as Lady Teazle, Beatrice, and Letitia Hardy. They made up for the shortage of stars with three novelties which must have strained the scenic department to the limit. On 1 September they presented Moncrieff's equestrian melodrama *The Cataract of the Ganges*; by 6 December it had had forty-two performances. *Cherry and Fair Star; or, The Children of Cyprus,* "a grand Asiatic Melodramatic Romance," opened 10 January and was as popular as the horse drama.[75] As a grand climax Weber's *Der Freischütz*, then the rage of London for its lovely music and exciting spectacle, opened 2 March and was repeated frequently during the rest of the season.[76]

Price was in London again in 1825. He had little difficulty persuading Edmund Kean to undertake a second American tour, for the tragedian was in bad odor with the London public as a result of his trial for adultery with the wife of Alderman Cox. When he made his first appearance at the Park, 14 November 1815, Kean was greeted with mingled approbation and abuse so general and so continued that little of the performance could be heard. His opponents objected to him on patriotic as well as moral grounds, remembering not only the episode of Mrs. Cox but also his refusal to act for an almost empty house in Boston in 1821, which had been blown up by the newspapers into arrogant disregard for American audiences in general. His second performance met little opposition, however, and he not only completed this engagement successfully but returned in February, May, and finally in November of 1826.[77] He did

[75] Odell, *Annals,* III, pp. 136, 144, 146.
[76] Odell, *Annals,* III, pp. 148, 149.
[77] Odell, *Annals,* III, pp. 178, 189, 196, 238.

very well, both for himself and for the management. Letters from William Clarke, Kean's private banker, acknowledge receipt from Simpson of £1450 in three payments, 31 January, 23 February, and 31 March.[78] He benefited from an improvement in economic conditions.

The last season for fourteen years in which Price dominated the Park management was notable for another attraction. Before Kean had finished his first engagement, Price presented the Garcia company in *The Barber of Seville*, the first long opera sung in New York in Italian or any other foreign language. Fitz-Greene Halleck told his biographer that this was due "to Signor Daponte [Lorenzo Da Ponte, Professor of Italian at Columbia] the personal friend of Mozart and writer of the libretto for 'Don Giovanni' and 'Le Nozze di Figaro,' he having with the late Dominick Lynch and Stephen Price induced the elder Garcia . . . with his troupe to appear at the Park Theatre."[79] The company consisted of the elder Garcia, first tenor; Mme. Garcia, soprano; the younger Garcia, baritone; their beautiful and talented daughter Maria, later famous throughout Europe as Mme. Malibran, contralto; Angrisani, basso; Crivelli, second tenor; and several others.[80] The chorus was picked up in New York.

From 29 November 1825 to 11 August 1826, the Garcia company gave seventy-nine performances of eight operas, five by Rossini, *Don Giovanni* by Mozart, and two by

[78] Edmund Kean, A.L.S., Folger.

[79] James Grant Wilson, *The Life and Letters of Fitz-Greene Halleck* (New York, 1869), p. 282. Scoville says that Lynch was a wine merchant, "an extensive importer and connoisseur of all nice things"— *The Old Merchants*, I, p. 169.

[80] Stirling Mackinlay, *Garcia the Centenarian and his Times* (London, 1908), lists four; the *Evening Post* (New York), 6 November 1826, lists six, only one of whom is mentioned by Mackinlay. Mackinlay's four, and one who appears nowhere else, are in Odell's abbreviated cast lists.

Garcia. Gross receipts were $56,685, an average of only $700 a night, despite the fact that ticket prices were doubled.[81] When we add the expense of chorus and augmented orchestra to what must have been the considerable sum paid to Garcia, we can be reasonably sure that Price and Simpson lost money on Italian opera, probably a good deal of money, but they gained prestige for the Park with New York's elite.

HITHERTO, Price had worked primarily in the United States, although, as has been seen, he made frequent trips to England. Beginning in 1826, with the Park firmly established as America's leading theatre, his activity as a producer shifted from New York to London. If he returned to the United States in the fall of 1825, he must have left again within a few months, for he was in London on 20 May 1826, when he responded to a toast at the Drury Lane Theatre Anniversary Dinner.[82] Thus, by accident or intention, he was on the ground when the lease of one of England's two great patent theatres became available early in June.

The actor Robert Elliston had leased the Theatre Royal, Drury Lane, in 1819 and had managed it satisfactorily until 5 August 1825, when he suffered a stroke. During the 1825-26 season, the theatre was managed by Elliston's son, advised by the playwright James Kenney and a committee of the proprietors.[83] Although Elliston recovered enough to act the following April, he was £5700 in arrears in the rent and owed substantial sums besides. On 3 June 1826, his lease was voided by the proprietors, and shortly afterwards he filed in bankruptcy.[84]

[81] Mackinlay, *Garcia*, p. 71; Odell, *Annals*, III, p. 182.

[82] *John Bull* (London), 21 May 1826.

[83] George Raymond, *The Life and Enterprises of Robert Wm. Elliston, Comedian* (London, 1857), p. 375.

[84] Report of Annual Meeting of Drury Lane Proprietors, unidentified

Three days later the proprietors advertised for sealed bids for terms of seven and fourteen years.[85] As early as 4 June it was rumored that Price would manage Drury Lane the following season, although the idea that a barbarous Yankee should direct one of London's major theatres was scoffed at as preposterous.[86]

When the bids were opened, it was discovered that Thomas Bish, Member of Parliament, "well-known on the Stock Exchange and as a lottery office keeper," was high bidder with a rental of £11,250 a year for fourteen years. Elliston had paid £10,200 a year.[87] A notice in the *Times* of 5 July requested that applications from performers seeking engagements at Drury Lane and "letters relating to the business of the theatre" be addressed to "the Manager, Stephen Price, esq." Apparently Price would manage the theatre for Bish.

That is not the end of the story. On 7 July Bish, who had not yet signed the final contract, notified the proprietors that he had changed his mind; he would not assume the lease. Instead of advertising again for bids, the proprietors awarded the lease to the second-highest bidder at a rental of £10,605 a year. The second-highest bidder was Stephen Price. Bish's £2000 deposit was assigned to Price in return for his assumption of contracts already made with actors and others. Among these were William Dunn, treasurer; James Winston, property man and house manager; James Wallack, stage manager; Frederic Reynolds, play reader; and Clarkson Stanfield, scene painter. The £2000, however,

---

clipping dated 4 July 1826, Drury Lane file, Enthoven Collection, Victoria and Albert Museum.

[85] *Chronicle* (London), 6 June 1826.

[86] *Age* (London), 4 June 1826.

[87] *John Bull* (London), 9 July 1826; Francis Place papers, MS, British Museum.

was held by the proprietors as a perpetual advance on the rent. In addition, Price put up £3000 of his own as surety.[88]

On the face of it, the maneuver suggests collusion between Bish and Price, but the situation may have been complicated by other factors. Winston, who disliked Price and recorded much to his discredit, says that Price was forced on Bish by a money-lender. Winston says also that the proprietors did not re-advertise for bids and transferred the lease to Price with the greatest secrecy to prevent anyone's taking the theatre on behalf of Elliston's creditors.[89]

Newspaper comments on the elevation of an American to the position of lessee and manager of Drury Lane were for the most part polite, but the *Age* on 9 July greeted the news with heavy sarcasm. It had earlier reacted with incredulity to the rumor that Price was to be manager. Now it declared, "With reference to Mr. Price, whose managerial talent we . . . ventured to question, we find ourselves quite mistaken. . . . We hear Master Stephen has been particularly active, and the very first day . . . in office, he engaged the principal tragedian, Mr. Macready, and the principal comedian, Mr. Elliston, for—HIS OWN THEATRE IN AMERICA —for which place HE HIMSELF STARTS ON THE 24TH OF THIS MONTH!! All this bids well for . . . Drury Lane." Price had indeed hired William Charles Macready for America, although most likely before he knew he was to be in charge at Drury Lane. He had made an offer to Elliston, or so Elliston said,[90] and he was preparing to cross the Atlantic himself.

[88] Minutes of the Annual Meeting of the Proprietors of Drury Lane Theatre, *Morning Chronicle* (London), 5 July 1827.

[89] MS notes dated 11 and 20 July 1826, James Winston, Drury Lane scrapbooks, XXIII, British Museum.

[90] Report of Annual Meeting of Drury Lane Proprietors, 4 July 1826, Enthoven.

He must have been very busy during the few days that remained to him in London. He offered starring engagements at Drury Lane to Charles Mathews and to Joseph Munden, another popular comedian.[91] Neither was available. In spite of the fact that Elliston claimed to have spent £50,000 on improvements to Drury Lane during his tenancy, the stage floor was in bad shape, and Price persuaded the proprietors to allow him £200 for a new one.[92] He must have arranged for the business of the theatre to be carried on in his absence. From newspaper reports, it appears that the responsibilities were shared by John Calcraft for the proprietors, William Dunn, James Wallack, Frederic Reynolds, and James Winston. This proxy management was looked on by the press as boding no good, for Drury Lane had been run by a committee of the proprietors from 1812 to 1819 with disastrous consequences.

On 22 July Price met Macready in Liverpool and concluded arrangements for his American tour, which was to begin at the Park Theatre in October.[93] Two days later Price sailed on the Corinthian. The voyage gave him plenty of time to rest, for the Corinthian did not reach New York until 3 September.[94]

Why did Price leave London almost as soon as he had secured the big prize of Drury Lane? Perhaps he needed to make new arrangements with Simpson regarding the management of the Park. Perhaps he needed to supply himself with funds to carry him through a possibly unprofitable first season at Drury Lane.

The Drury Lane Theatre which Price had acquired was

[91] Mathews, *Memoirs*, III, p. 572; A.L.S., Price to Munden, Harvard Theatre Collection.

[92] MS note, Winston scrapbooks, XXIII, BM.

[93] *Macready's Reminiscences and Diaries*, ed. Sir Frederick Pollock (New York, 1875), p. 223.

[94] *Evening Post* (New York), 4 and 5 September 1826.

the fourth to stand on the Brydges Street site. Constructed in 1812, it was 131 feet wide and 237 feet long, not including 93 feet of shops. It seated 3060 in three tiers of public boxes, proscenium and private boxes, pit, two galleries, and slips.[95] The shape of the auditorium was very nearly that of a horseshoe. The proscenium was 46 feet 6 inches wide, 43 feet high, and 12 feet 6 inches deep to the front curtain. There were no proscenium doors. From the center boxes to the front curtain was 48 feet; from the orchestra to the back wall of the stage was 96 feet 3 inches.[96]

The auditorium was illuminated by a huge cut-glass chandelier lighted by gas and hung from the center of the domed ceiling, and by wax candles in small cut-glass chandeliers hung from brackets attached to the iron shafts which supported the second and third tiers of boxes. The stage was lighted by gas.[97]

At the advertised prices—boxes 7s., pit 3s.6d., lower gallery 2s., and upper gallery 1s.—the house could produce between £600 and £700, although on occasion it could be made to yield more. Fixed expenses, if we may take these as indicated by the benefit charges, were nearly £250.[98] There were three other sources of revenue: the box-office concession for the sale of food and drink, £300 a year; the great-coat (checkroom) concession, £100 a year; and receipts from the sale of playbills and books of the play which were printed on a private press in a room below the stage, £100 to £200 a year.[99]

---

[95] Horace Foote, *A Companion to the Theatres* (London, 1828), p. 36; unidentified clipping dated 27 July 1827, Winston scrapbooks, XXIII.

[96] Foote, *Companion to the Theatres*, pp. 35, 37; Charles Dibdin, Jun., *History and Illustrations of the London Theatres* (London, 1826), pp. 63, 65.

[97] Foote, *Companion*, pp. 36, 37, 129.

[98] Foote, *Companion*, p. 132.   [99] Drury Lane Ledger, Folger.

A number of factors reduced the actual nightly income. Regularly at nine o'clock at the end of the third act of the main play, customers were admitted at half-price. Thirty-five private boxes, each of which held six to eight persons, were rented by the season for prices averaging about 25s. a night for each entire box.[100] One group of the proprietors, the "new renters," who had contributed to the construction of the building in 1812, were entitled to free admission to the public boxes. There was a considerable "free list" consisting of representatives of the newspapers and magazines which published theatre news and criticism.[101] The principal actors had at their disposal orders for free admission. The manager and the treasurer too issued such orders. Dunn was said to pay off his women regularly in this currency. Orders were issued on the afternoon of performance, the number depending on how many box admissions had been sold.[102]

Consequently, newspaper reports of attendance can be misleading. For example, they reported a full house for the first performance under the new management on 23 September. According to Winston, attendance totaled 2102, a good house but not full. Of these, 998 paid full price, 838 half-price, and 266 were admitted free. £268 was taken at the door.[103]

The opening of Drury Lane for the 1826-27 season was notable only for the London debut of Ellen Tree as Violante in Mrs. Centlivre's comedy *The Wonder*. Miss Tree was twenty years old, just beginning the long career in which

[100] Winston scrapbooks, XXIII, BM.

[101] Drury Lane Ledger, Folger.

[102] Henry Philipps, *Musical and Personal Reminiscences During Half a Century*, 2 vols. (London, 1864), I, p. 243.

[103] Winston scrapbooks, XXIII, BM. The Drury Lane Ledger at the Folger records £248.19s.

she rose to the head of her profession. She remained at Drury Lane for three seasons under Price's management, gaining valuable experience.

With few exceptions, the bills for the first weeks presented the stock company in standard plays and operas. One exception was the revival on 28 September of Weber's *Der Freischütz*, with "The Scenery, Dresses, Machinery, etc. entirely new."[104] Another was the premiere on 9 October of Boiledieu's musical drama *The White Lady*, with English words. It was praised only for its scenery, "such as poets may dream of and only Stanfield realize," one critic declared.[105] Receipts for the first thirty-five performances, through 11 November, averaged only £175, seriously under expenses.[106] Old Drury was doing poorly in Price's absence. Price had arrived in New York on 3 September.[107] He dined with Philip Hone, wealthy merchant and former mayor, on 7 September, and, presumably having completed his business, sailed for England again on 13 September.[108] He arrived at Liverpool on 8 October, and returned to Drury Lane Theatre, according to a note by James Winston, "Wed'y 11 Oct. 26 at 1/2 past ten."[109]

The press looked for better things at Drury Lane with King Stephen on his throne. Hope was expressed that he would combat the evil of "starring." It had been reported with approval that Price intended to form a company "at fixed salaries" without stars.[110] The severe financial difficul-

---

[104] Playbill, BM.

[105] *New Monthly Magazine* (London), 1 November 1826, p. 454.

[106] Drury Lane Ledger, Folger.

[107] *Evening Post* (New York), 4 September 1826.

[108] MS Diary, I, 40, NYHS; *Evening Post* (New York), 14 September 1826.

[109] *News* (London), 15 November 1826; Winston scrapbooks, XXIII, BM.

[110] *John Bull* (London), 15 October 1826.

ties of Drury Lane and Covent Garden were due in part to
competition from the half-dozen minor theatres licensed to
present everything except standard drama, and even more
to the general hard times. England was suffering the economic depression that followed the financial panic of
December 1825. But several commentators blamed the
practice recently initiated by Robert Elliston of paying
leading actors by the performance, instead of by the week
like the rest of the company.

It is doubtful, however, that Price considered doing without stars at Drury Lane. He had learned how attractive
they could be at the Park and, in spite of their cost, how
profitable. Among his first actions as manager was to make
starring offers to Mathews and Munden. They were un-
available, but he secured others, as will be seen. Later in his
management, when he attempted to save on salaries, he did
not cut down on stars.

John Braham, "the King of British Song,"[111] whom Price
had wanted for America, began a long starring engagement
at Drury Lane on 21 October. Pierre-François Laporte, a
talented French comedian, made his first appearance in
November. In December, Catherine Stephens, the sweet-
faced singer who was to leave the stage in 1838 to marry the
fifth Earl of Essex, strengthened the company in opera, and
Joseph Liston, eccentric comedian, second perhaps only to
Charles Mathews, joined Laporte, John Harley, and William Dowton to make Drury Lane very strong in farce.
Braham, Laporte, Stephens, and Liston were all paid by the
performance.

Business improved after Price's return, but not much. For
the thirty-five performances from 12 November through
22 December, receipts averaged £190, including £915 on

111 *Literary Gazette* (London), 6 June 1829.

1 December when King George IV made his annual visit to Drury Lane.[112] This was still under expenses.

For the King's command performance, no orders were issued. John Liston made a special trip from Brighton, where he was finishing a provincial tour, to oblige His Majesty, who wished to see him as Lubin Log in James Kenney's farce *Love, Law, and Physick*. Any democratic scruples Stephen Price may have felt did not prevent him from donning court dress and, with Wallack and Winston, greeting His Majesty at the theatre entrance and lighting the way with candles to the apartment adjoining the royal box.[113]

Receipts began to rise above expenses with the Christmas pantomime, *Man in the Moon; or, Harlequin Dog-Star*, a lavish mixture of spectacular scenery, special music, tricks, transformations, fantastic costumes, dancing, juggling, and tightrope walking. It opened, as was the custom, on 26 December and received favorable reviews.[114]

But it was the return of Edmund Kean after his season in America that really turned the tide. He opened as Shylock on 8 January to a full and enthusiastic house. One observer reported that when the curtain rose, "There was one unbroken yell for Kean, which drowned all other sounds."[115] Kean played three nights a week in his accustomed roles. Price paid him £50 a night,[116] which was a lot of money when the most an actor on salary could command was £20 a week. But Kean was worth every penny of it. In his first

[112] Drury Lane Ledger, Folger.
[113] Unidentified clipping hand-dated December 1826, Winston scrapbooks, XXIII, BM.
[114] Playbill, BM; *John Bull* (London), 31 December 1826; *New Monthly Magazine*, 1 February 1827.
[115] *Opera Glass* (London), 13 January 1827.
[116] Receipt, Folger.

fifteen nights, receipts averaged £478.[117] For the first time this season, Drury Lane was operating in the black.

A highlight of the spring was the first appearance of the charming and accomplished singing actress Mary Ann Paton, as Mandane in Thomas Arne's popular opera *Artaxerxes*. Miss Paton, whose love-life was as much discussed in 1827 as Elizabeth Taylor's has been in our time, was then more or less secretly married to Lord William Pitt Lennox, a young man about town. The marriage was dissolved in 1831, Miss Paton married the singer Joseph Wood, and the couple had a long and successful career. In 1827 Miss Paton was under contract to Covent Garden, and her appearance at Drury Lane suggests shrewd maneuvering by Price. Ordinarily, Catherine Stephens would have sung Mandane, but she pleaded illness. Price persuaded Miss Paton to help him out with this one performance. She failed to secure permission from Covent Garden and her contract was voided, permitting Price to secure her for a limited engagement in May and for further engagements the following season.

In May, also, Edmund Kean returned for a second engagement after touring the provinces. He had felt for some time that he must add a new role to his repertory if he were not to risk gradually losing his audience. From several plays submitted to him by Price, he selected Henry Grattan's tragedy *Ben Nazir*,[118] and a good deal of interest was aroused by the announcement that Kean would appear in the title role. On 21 May he stumbled through it, able to remember only a few of the lines. The audience laughed at scenes intended to be serious. At the end of the perform-

---

[117] *News* (London), 13 May 1827; *Age* (London), 20 May 1827.
[118] Brian Waller Procter, *The Life of Edmund Kean*, 2 vols. (London, 1835), II, pp. 267-268.

ance, James Wallack in his capacity as stage manager came before the curtain and apologized for Kean, "sick in body, and harassed in mind, his memory, his once powerful memory had betrayed its trust."[119] Some blamed the playwright, more blamed the actor, but all agreed that it was a disaster. Kean managed to finish his engagement in familiar roles, although he was often far from himself because of illness or drink or both.

After the last performance on 30 June the *Literary Gazette* commented, "The energies and abilities of Mr. Price have brought the season at this unfortunate theatre to a prosperous close."[120] The proprietors had reason to be pleased. Price had paid the rent promptly for 212 nights, twelve more than the minimum for which he had contracted.[121] Consequently, the new renters had received their 1s.6d. a night, the ground rent had been paid to the Duke of Bedford, all other bills had been paid, and the bonded debt reduced from £19,184 to £14,821. Until the bonded debt was paid off, the original shareholders received nothing.[122]

It was reported that Price had profited by about £6000 by the season, while his rivals at Covent Garden had lost about the same sum.[123] He probably did not do nearly that well. The Drury Lane Ledger appears to show an excess of receipts over expenditures of about £2300, but it does not strike a balance, and one cannot be sure that all expenses are shown. For instance, I find no salary for Reynolds, Price's playreader. The manager's own page in the Ledger shows payments and receipts of £2800 exactly balanced.

[119] *Literary Gazette* (London), 26 May 1827.
[120] Undated clipping, Drury Lane playbills, BM.
[121] Drury Lane Ledger, Folger.
[122] Report of Annual Meeting of the Proprietors of Drury Lane, *Morning Chronicle* (London), 5 July 1827.
[123] *Age* (London), 1 July 1827.

Price's exertions at Drury Lane may have led him to neglect the Park, for business was miserable there during the 1827-28 season. In April 1828, the management offered to sell the lease, properties, and fixtures "to an association of gentlemen or a joint stock company."[124] Apparently there were no takers. Perhaps prospects improved with the destruction by fire on 26 May of the rival Bowery Theatre. At any rate, on 1 September Simpson renewed the lease at an annual rental of $16,000.[125]

For the 1827-28 season at Drury Lane, Price announced Macready, returning from his first American tour; Mary Ann Paton; Emma Love, another charming and scandalous singing actress; and Richard Jones, an accomplished comedian. All except Macready were from Covent Garden, a considerable raid on the talent of the rival theatre.

The Covent Garden management struck back. Late in July it became known that Kean, who had been a pillar of Drury Lane since his debut there in 1814, would appear in the fall at Covent Garden. Price and Kean had failed to agree. Perhaps, as one newspaper suggested, Kean was unwilling to share the stage with Macready.[126]

Price was not to be bested easily. He hired Henry Bishop, England's leading composer and conductor, to direct the operas.[127] He persuaded Charles Mathews to accept a starring engagement on what Mrs. Mathews called extravagantly liberal terms.[128] He signed Maria Foote, a young actress with a small talent for comedy, great personal charm, and considerable notoriety.[129] With the Misses

124 *Albion* (New York), 19 April 1828.
125 Porter, *John Jacob Astor*, II, p. 990.
126 *John Bull* (London), 12 August 1827.
127 *Age* (London), 12 August 1827. Bishop was knighted in 1842, the first musician to be so honored.
128 Mathews, *Memoirs*, III, p. 294.
129 *John Bull* (London), 26 August 1827.

Paton, Love, and Foote, Price could present three of the most attractive women on the London stage. Only Madame Vestris was lacking for a monopoly of feminine charm.

Meantime it was rumored that Price was preparing something really extraordinary. With the publication of the opening playbill on 22 September the well-kept secret was out. "Mr. Kean, Jun.," the sixteen-year-old son of the great Edmund, was engaged to play at Drury Lane.[130]

Young Charles Kean had been at Eton receiving a gentleman's education when his father, in financial difficulties, obtained for him the offer of a clerkship in the East India Company. Price sent Wallack to Eton to persuade Charles to accept instead an engagement acting at Drury Lane for three years. Encouraged by his mother, who was separated from Edmund, the young man determined to try his luck on the stage.[131] Edmund did not want his son to become an actor, and it was rumored that he had applied to the Lord Chamberlain for an injunction to prevent Charles from performing at Drury Lane.

Needless to say, all this created considerable furore, and Drury Lane was "crammed to suffocation" when Charles Kean made his debut as Young Norval in Home's tragedy *Douglas*.[132] The audience received him warmly, but most of the reviewers were not so charitable. They found in Charles no signs of his father's genius, and marked defects in voice and movement. The *News* of 7 October called his performance "the Norval of a schoolboy," which no doubt it was, and the *Times* of 2 October advised him, if it was not too late, to accept the clerkship in the East India Company.

Charles was discouraged, naturally enough. He wanted

130 Playbill, BM.
131 J. W. Cole, *The Life and Theatrical Times of Charles Kean*, 2 vols. (London, 1859), I, p. 149.
132 *Age* (London), 7 October 1827.

to cancel his engagement, but Price urged him to persevere and declined to let him off.[133] Perhaps Price detected signs of the talent that eventually made Charles Kean a star in a style different from that of his father. More likely, he kept the young man because he was an attraction. It was reported that his debut drew £600,[134] and that in the first two weeks he put £1400 in the manager's pocket.[135]

The more substantial attractions, Jones, Miss Paton, and Miss Foote, followed Charles Kean at intervals. Macready returned and appeared first as Macbeth on 12 November. As usual, the critics were divided about his ability to play Shakespeare, although they were enthusiastic about his acting in Knowles' *Virginius* and other contemporary verse plays. He did not attract audiences, and although he was contracted for forty nights at £20 a night, he left the company after sixteen performances. Price paid him £320 for the remaining twenty-four nights.[136] Macready never forgave Price for this indignity.

December was marked by another failure in tragedy, one which must have been particularly painful to Price. Thomas A. Cooper, for over a quarter of a century the leading actor of the American stage, and Price's old friend and former partner, appeared at Drury Lane on 17 December as Macbeth. The audience laughed at his final scene, most of the critics dealt severely with his performance, and although he was announced for Othello he returned to America without having appeared again.[137]

Other attractions compensated for these disappointments. The Christmas pantomime, *Harlequin and Cock Robin,* was

[133] Cole, *Life of Charles Kean,* I, p. 152.
[134] *Age* (London), 7 October 1827.
[135] *News* (London), 14 October 1827.
[136] Drury Lane Ledger, Folger.
[137] *Literary Gazette* (London), 22 December 1827; *Age* (London), 3 February 1828; unidentified clipping, Drury Lane playbills, Enthoven.

a success.[138] Charles Mathews began his long engagement on 31 December as Sir Fretful Plagiary in Sheridan's *The Critic*.[139] The critics differed regarding his merits in the role, but he drew large houses. When he played Sir Fretful, with Liston as Don Whiskerandos, and Buskin in Theodore Hook's farce *Killing No Murder*, receipts were reported to have exceeded £550.[140] This was an exaggeration, but Mathews' nights averaged £451.[141]

Mary Ann Duff, who had achieved considerable reputation as a tragedienne in the United States, made her London debut at Drury Lane on 3 March 1828, in the title role of Southerne's tragedy *Isabella*. Doubtless because of Cooper's experience, she was billed as from the Theatre Royal, Dublin.[142] She was well received by audience and critics,[143] but she did not appear again until 4 April, this time as the pathetic Adelgitha. Again she was well received. In spite of the fact that Price needed a tragic actress, she did not appear again. Ireland says that she and Price could not agree on salary and she was not paid.[144] The Ledger shows no payment.

At the end of the season, Price won general goodwill by offering Drury Lane for a benefit on 27 June to Joe Grimaldi, now old and ailing. Covent Garden, where Grimaldi had played for many years, was denied him.[145]

The 1827-28 season was apparently a success. When the proprietors met in July, they were informed that the rent had been paid for 212 performances and Price's deposit was

138 *News* (London), 30 December 1827.

139 Playbill, BM.

140 Unidentified clipping, hand-dated 20 January 1828, Winston scrapbooks, xxiii, BM.

141 Drury Lane Ledger, Folger.   142 Playbill, BM.

143 *Age* (London), 9 March 1828.

144 Joseph N. Ireland, *Mrs. Duff* (Boston, 1882), p. 50.

145 Playbill, BM.

intact. The new renters and all bills had been paid, and the bonded debt had been reduced to £11,161.[146]

All was not well, nevertheless. Price had pressed the proprietors to protect the patent rights of Drury Lane against increasing encroachment by the minor theatres. In February 1828 they brought suit against George Davidge, manager of the Coburg, for two unauthorized performances, one of Home's *Douglas*, one of *Macbeth*, and on 30 July a jury awarded them £200 in damages. The proprietors had to pay their own costs, however.[147]

Price attempted to provide for the Park's 1828-29 season by sending James Wallack off to America, thus depriving Drury Lane of one of its most useful actors. John Cooper assumed Wallack's duties as stage manager.

At Drury Lane the bill announcing the opening of the 1828-29 season revealed some major changes. Miss Paton and Miss Foote were missing from the list of stars. Braham and Liston were re-engaged, but Mathews was not to be persuaded. He found acting in huge Drury Lane too great a strain.[148]

From Covent Garden Price secured William Farren, who was much admired by the critics in the line of old men in standard comedy. Charles Kemble for Covent Garden sued Farren for breach of contract and eventually won £750 damages, which Price paid. Charles M. Young's contract lapsed at Covent Garden and Price signed this leading tragic actor. Young was past his prime, and his style was somewhat out of fashion, but with him Price could occasionally present a standard tragedy. Mrs. Bunn, the nearest thing to a tragedy queen the English stage had been able

[146] Report of Annual Meeting of Proprietors of Drury Lane Theatre, *Morning Chronicle* (London), 12 July 1828.

[147] *Times* (London), 31 July 1828.

[148] Playbill, BM.

to offer since Mrs. Siddons retired, was engaged to team with Young. For the first time under Price's management, Drury Lane was reasonably well staffed for tragedy.

The 1828-29 season was notable less for stars than for new productions. On 9 October Price presented the premiere of *Rienzi*, a new verse tragedy by Mary Russell Mitford, with Young in the title role. The play is laid in fourteenth-century Rome and centers on Rienzi, a proud and independent man who leads a successful rebellion against the tyrannous Ursini, becomes a tyrant himself, and dies by the spears of a new generation of rebels. He is a Napoleon, a superman. The reviewers analyzed the play and the performances at length and had little but praise for both. They agreed that Young had outdone himself. The *Stage* called his performance "one of the proudest triumphs of his art."[149] In the ingenue role of Claudia, Rienzi's daughter, Price gambled on a sixteen-year-old unknown, Louisa Ann Phillips. She was praised for naturalness and elegance. In succeeding months Price presented her as Juliet and in other standard roles. *Rienzi* played thirty-four performances, the last on 25 May—a genuine hit.[150] Miss Mitford was paid £200.[151]

This was only the beginning. On 24 October Ellen Tree, who had sunk into obscurity after her first season, achieved a personal triumph in the title role of *The Youthful Queen; or, Christine of Sweden*, a new "petite comedy" by Charles Shannon.[152] *The Youthful Queen* played seventeen performances.[153] Even more successful was J. R. Planché's new historical drama *Charles XII; or, The Siege of Stralsund*, which opened on 11 December and played forty-nine per-

---

[149] *The Stage, or Theatrical Inquisitor* (London), 1 (October, 1828).
[150] Playbills, BM.   [151] Drury Lane Ledger, Folger.
[152] *Literary Gazette* (London), 1 November 1828.
[153] Summary of the Season, Drury Lane file, Enthoven.

formances. The *Literary Gazette*, 11 December 1828, called it "a genuine picture of the times, admirably embodied, and strikingly carried into action."

The Christmas pantomime was praised. *The Queen Bee; or, Harlequin and the Fairy Hive* had something for everyone except the lover of literature: James Barnes, the best Pantaloon of the day; the "surprising Foreign Dwarf"; and above all a "New Diorama and Grand Moving Picture" by Clarkson Stanfield. A whole second sheet of playbill was required to detail the wonders of Stanfield's creation.[154] Spectacular scenery contributed also to the success in April of *Thiera-Na-Oge; or, The Prince of the Lakes*, a concoction by Planché and William Barrymore, billed as "A Grand Melodramatic Fairy Tale."[155]

Price had begun the season with a successful new tragedy; he ended it with a successful new opera, Auber's *Masaniello; or, The Dumb Girl of Portici*. For this production, which opened on 4 May, no expense was spared. Madame Alexandrine of the Paris Opera was imported to play the dumb girl, band and chorus were augmented, and spectacular scenery was provided. According to one reviewer, Braham "gave his 'whole soul' to the title role," and "The only performer at all imperfect on the first night was Mt. Vesuvius, which in its final eruption sent up more smoke than fire."[156] The playbill for 5 May announced that *Masaniello* would be repeated every night except Saturday; the playbill for 12 May added Saturday, with the admonition, "And all Orders totally suspended!" By the end of the season *Masaniello* had played twenty-three performances without exhausting its popularity.[157]

[154] Playbill, Walter Hampden Library, The Players.
[155] Playbill, BM.
[156] "Historical Register," *New Monthly Magazine* (June, 1829), p. 246.
[157] Playbills, BM.

In spite of these hits, the season had not gone well financially. As early as 6 March, Price had written to Wallack in
Philadelphia: "Our season has been more successful than
profitable. We stand very far ahead in our receipt and
popularity, but the immense expense of the unemployed
members of a patent theatre are enough to ruin it."[158] He
was discovering how many actors could be idled by hits.

It is significant that the season ended a week earlier than
usual and that Price was licensed by the Lord Chamberlain
to hold two "Masquerades" at Drury Lane for his benefit on
15 and 29 June.[159] A Masquerade was a kind of low-class
night club on a large scale, combining dancing, entertainment, food, and drink. Price's name did not appear in connection with these two Masquerades; he gave them over for
£1000 to Charles Wright, who held the box-office concession at Drury Lane.[160]

When minutes of the annual meeting of the proprietors
were published, it was clear that Price was in financial
difficulty. Although he had paid the rent and the new
renters had received their 1s.6d. a night, the proprietors
had agreed to return to Price the rental for thirty-six nights,
amounting to £1800. In response to a question John Calcraft, who presided, said that Price had lost several
thousand pounds since February.[161]

Price attempted to improve his position before the opening of the 1829-30 season. By weeding out actors on weekly
salary, he was reported to have reduced expenses by
£3000.[162] He reduced admission to the boxes to 6s., hoping

[158] A.L.S., Harvard Theatre Collection.
[159] Register of Licenses, Public Record Office, London.
[160] Winston scrapbooks, XXIII, BM.
[161] *Morning Chronicle* (London), 5 July 1829.
[162] Unidentified clipping hand-dated 26 September 1829, Winston
scrapbooks, XXIII, BM.

this would increase attendance.[163] He did not economize on leading actors, however. Braham, Liston, Farren, Jones, Young, Miss Stephens, Miss Phillips, and Mrs. Bunn were re-engaged. James Wallack returned from America.

The season opened on 1 October, with Young as Hamlet; Mrs. Faucit, returning after five years, as Gertrude; and Miss Faucit in her London debut as Ophelia. The next night Ducrow, an acrobat and equestrian, represented a sequence of well-known statues in "The Living Model of the Antiques," an extra attraction for six nights. On 9 October, John Sinclair, singing actor and composer, began a starring engagement.[164]

But none of these could compete with the bright new star that had risen at Covent Garden. Fanny Kemble, daughter of actor-manager Charles Kemble and niece of Sarah Siddons, made her debut on 5 October as Juliet and created a sensation. The rush to see her filled Covent Garden on Mondays, Wednesdays, and Fridays.

The London debut of Miss Mordaunt, later Mrs. Nisbett, a vivacious comedienne, and the return after five years of Mrs. Glover, an accomplished actress in tragedy and comedy, did not swing the balance back to Drury Lane. On 6 November, the principal actors agreed to forego one-quarter of their salaries for ten weeks, by the end of which it was hoped business would be better.[165]

Then Price played what he must have hoped was a trump card. The playbill for 27 November announced that Edmund Kean would appear at Drury Lane on 30 November and regularly thereafter on Mondays, Wednesdays, and Fridays—Fanny Kemble's nights at Covent Garden.

[163] Playbill, BM.   [164] Playbills, BM.
[165] Unidentified clipping dated 11 November 1829, Winston scrapbooks, XXIII, BM.

Charles Kemble, who believed that Kean had agreed to act in London only at Covent Garden, applied for and was granted an injunction restraining Kean from appearing at Drury Lane. Price's attorneys immediately moved successfully to lift the injunction, and Kean returned to Drury Lane on 2 December to a crowded house.[166]

The various facets of the agreement between Kean and Kemble, as reported in the newspapers, are too complex to recite here, but it seems likely that Price, guessing that Kean would not care to share the Covent Garden stage with Fanny Kemble, sent John Cooper to woo the star back to Drury Lane, and that Kean took advantage of the looseness of his agreement with Kemble to escape his obligation.[167]

Price scored too with his Christmas pantomime *Jack in the Box*, in large part because of the spectacular scenery, particularly Stanfield's "Grand Local Diorama" which presented views of London and Windsor and "The Magnificent Display of the Falls of the Virginia Waters, seen through the Fairy Temple of Luminaria."[168] An observer reported: "About 70 tons of water fall down from a height of between 30 and 40 feet, and are conducted in a meandering course to the bottom of the stage, whence by an ingenious contrivance, they descend to the main sewer."[169]

In January Madame Vestris, the most popular comedienne and singing actress of the day, began a starring engagement at Drury Lane. She contributed a good deal to the success of *The National Guard*, a new comic opera adapted from Auber and Scribe which opened on 4 February.[170]

[166] *Literary Gazette* (London), 12 December 1829.
[167] *News* (London), 6 December 1829. See also Harold N. Hillebrand, *Edmund Kean* (New York, 1933), pp. 305-307.
[168] Playbill, Walter Hampden Library, The Players.
[169] *Times* (London), 25 December 1829.
[170] Playbills, BM.

Vestris and Kean drew good houses when they were able to play, but she was plagued by hoarseness and he by generally failing health. In spite of Kean's condition, he was announced to appear 22 February as Henry V, a new role. A last-minute announcement that he was too ill to act caused a near-riot.[171] When he attempted the part two weeks later, the *News* reported that he made a pitiful appearance and could not speak six consecutive lines.[172]

By this time, however, Kean's condition could hardly have mattered to Price. For several months rumors had circulated that the manager was ill and in grave financial trouble. These were confirmed when in the middle of March the proprietors voided Price's lease and announced that James Wallack would manage Drury Lane for the remainder of the season.[173] Price had failed in the rent to the amount of £1800 over his deposit, but he had paid all he owed to actors and tradespeople for services to the theatre.[174] He had borrowed £1000 from the actor John Cooper[175] and more than that amount from Frederic Reynolds.[176] Doubtless he owed others. Notice of his petition for bankruptcy appeared in the *Times* 8 July, and bankruptcy was granted as of 26 September.[177]

How much Price lost in his management of Drury Lane can only be conjectured. The *Age* for 30 June reported that receipts had averaged £53,000 a season and, assuming that expenses were £250 a night for two hundred nights, Price had a profit of £3000 a season. Therefore, his bankruptcy

171 *Times* (London), 23 February 1830.

172 14 March 1830.

173 *Age* (London), 14 March 1830.

174 Report of Annual Meeting of the Proprietors of Drury Lane Theatre, *Morning Chronicle* (London), 5 July 1830.

175 Winston, MS note, December 1829, John Cooper folder, Folger.

176 MS note, 4 May 1830, Winston scrapbooks, XXIII, BM.

177 *United Kingdom Gazette*, 26 August 1830.

must have been due to losses elsewhere. John Cooper told Winston that Price's first three seasons averaged £53,000 and that Price was involved with a money-lender.[178] The Drury Lane Ledger appears to show for the first season a surplus of £2300, for the second a deficit of £5000. For the third season, Price may have broken even; both receipts and expenses were down. It is impossible to strike a balance for the fourth season, but receipts were down £4000 from the third season. The Ledger includes under separate headings Price's debits and credits. He paid in £1737 more than he withdrew. If this figure can be accepted and the £3000 Price put up as surety is added to it, King Stephen lost £4737.

After his bankruptcy, Price remained in England nearly a year hiring performers for the Park. When he returned to New York in August 1831[179] he was received as an absentee landlord. He was blamed for the Park's financial difficulties, and he was accused by supporters of the rival Bowery Theatre of having acquired anti-American views during his five years abroad. The anti-British sentiment which produced a riotous demonstration against Joshua Anderson on his debut at the Park on 13 October was directed in part against Price. The fact that the Park had presented, on 26 September, the premiere of *The Gladiator* by the American playwright Robert Montgomery Bird and that the American star Edwin Forrest had been a great success as Spartacus had not sufficed to silence those who complained that Price had turned the Park into a carbon copy of Drury Lane.

Although business at the Park was not good—it reflected the country's general economic condition—Price sailed for

[178] MS notes, dated 9 May 1830 and 11 January 1829, Winston scrapbooks, XXIII, BM.

[179] *Evening Post* (New York), 10 August 1831.

Stephen Price

Portion of a playbill for *Der Freischütz*, at the Park Theatre

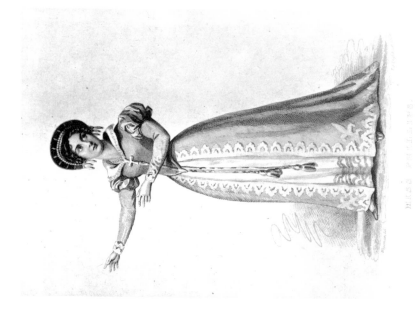

Louisa Ann Phillips as Claudio in *Pizarro*

John Braham, center, in the title role in *Masaniello*

Fanny Elssler dancing "La Tarantelle"

Edwin Booth as Hamlet

Romeo and Juliet at Booth's Theatre on opening night

Scene from Wyndham's revival of *David Garrick* at the Criterion

Wyndham's farewell performance in *Rosemary*

England again late in January, arriving in Liverpool on 17 February.[180] In London he discharged all his debts to the amount of several thousand pounds, although as a bankrupt he was no longer responsible for them.[181] Presumably he had sold property in New York to make this possible. It was more than a gesture; a reputation for financial integrity was essential to Price as London agent for the Park, in which he retained a half-interest.[182]

He now had to compete with Francis Wemyss from Philadelphia, James Caldwell from New Orleans, and Thomas Hamblin from the Bowery Theatre in New York, all of whom visited London periodically in search of performers and plays.

The Park needed the best Price could provide. In August 1832 Simpson was behind in the rent, and this time Astor indulged him because business in general was so depressed.[183]

Price did well during the next six years, sending across the Atlantic James Wallack; Louisa Ann Phillips, whom he had discovered at Drury Lane; Mlle. Augusta, a dancer from the Paris Opera; William Dowton, J. S. Balls, John Reeve, and Mr. and Mrs. Robert Keeley, all comic actors; Mme. Caradori Allen, singing actress; Mr. and Mrs. Joseph Wood; Charles Mathews for his second American tour; Ellen Tree, another discovery of Price's at Drury Lane; Tyrone Power, specialist in Irish characters; and Charles and Fanny Kemble.

Except for poor old Dowton, well past his prime, all had some success at the Park. Tyrone Power was so popular in 1832-34 that Price engaged him in 1836 and again in 1840. But the greatest success was that of the Kembles in 1832-34.

[180] *Morning Chronicle* (London), 13 and 20 February 1832.
[181] *Morning Post* (London), 27 February 1832.
[182] A.L.S., Price to Simpson, 14 December 1832, Folger.
[183] Letter, Astor to Beekman, 4 August 1832, Porter, *John Jacob Astor*, II, p. 1217.

For the sixty nights of their several engagements at the Park, receipts averaged $922. They were equally popular in other cities. Francis Wemyss credited them with restoring the American theatre to prosperity.[184] In fact, they must share the credit with an improvement in the national economy between 1832 and 1835.

Price accompanied Tyrone Power on his first trip to America, arriving in New York 2 August 1833.[185] He remained long enough to boast to Philip Hone that he had paid off all his debts in England,[186] and to refuse the Park Theatre to Thomas Cooper for a benefit on his retirement. Price may have turned against his old friend because in his later years Cooper had acted at the Chatham and Bowery as well as at the Park. King Stephen was back in London in time to attend the Anniversary Dinner of the Garrick Club on 4 February 1834. He had been a member of that convivial organization since 1832.[187]

The fortunes of the Park Theatre began to decline again in the season of 1835-36 as a result of the financial depression which culminated in the panic of 1837. Its prospects were further darkened when James Wallack, so long associated with the Park as visiting star, assumed the management of the National Theatre in New York. Price never forgave him for this.

To combat that competition, Price in June or July of 1838 signed Madame Vestris and Charles James Mathews for a year's engagement to begin at the Park in September. Although Vestris was no longer young she was still much admired, and young Mathews had gained recognition for

184 *Theatrical Biography* (Glasgow, 1848), p. 182.

185 *Standard* (New York), 21 August 1833; Tyrone Power, *Impressions of America During the Years 1833, 1834, and 1835*, 2 vols. (London, 1836), I, p. 47.

186 Hone MS Diary, VII, 22 August 1833, NYHS.

187 Extracts from Minutes, 1831-36, Garrick Club.

his skill in a new style of comic acting. For two seasons at
the Olympic Theatre under Vestris's management, the pair
had attracted an elite audience in refined comedy and
burlesque produced with taste and with unusual attention
to detail.[188]

The couple had not only co-starred but for several years
had cohabited quite openly without the formality of marriage. A few days before they sailed for America, the relationship was legalized in a ceremony that was kept secret
until they were on the high seas.[189] It was generally believed that Price had forced them to marry because he
thought Americans would not accept them while they were
living in sin. When Mathews and Vestris opened at the Park
Theatre in September, audiences were unenthusiastic. They
met a similar reception in Philadelphia, and after a second
engagement at the Park in October they returned to England, having fulfilled only two months of their twelve-
month contract.[190]

Several factors combined to produce this disaster. Vestris
and young Mathews had developed a new style of acting,
more refined, less exaggerated than that of the elder
Mathews, Liston, and others of the older generation. Given
a little time, American audiences might have learned to
appreciate it, but puritanism and patriotism combined to
deny the stars a fair hearing. Women stayed away from
their performances to show their disapproval of the actors'
morals.[191] Others boycotted them because they were said
to be anti-American. The Mathewses had arrived early in
August, and to escape the heat spent several days at a hotel
in the Catskills. There not only did they eat their meals in

[188] *Age* (London), 3 June 1838.
[189] *Examiner* (London), 22 July 1838.
[190] Odell, *Annals*, IV, pp. 273-274, 278.
[191] Odell, *Annals*, IV, p. 273.

their own quarters but they sent their servants to the public dining room.[192] Several newspapers inimical to the Park Theatre construed this as an expression of contempt for Americans.

Altogether, 1838-39 was a bad season for the Park, and Price set to work with his usual energy to make 1839-40 much better. In spite of competition from Wallack, who was in London in June 1839 recruiting for the National Theatre, Price succeeded in re-engaging Tyrone Power and J. S. Balls, both of whom had done well on previous tours. He also hired Fanny Fitzwilliam, a charming and versatile comedienne, and several singing actors. But these were not the biggest guns in the campaign in which he hoped to overcome all opposition and restore the Park to pre-eminence. Early in July, with the help of Henry Wikoff, a wealthy young American living in Paris, he engaged Fanny Elssler of the Paris Opera, the most famous and admired dancer of the day. For thirty-six nights at the Park in the spring of 1840, Miss Elssler was to receive half of the receipts after a deduction of $150 a night, except for her benefit nights, when she was to receive half of the gross receipts.[193]

When Price sailed for New York in the late summer of 1839 he must have hoped to set things right at the Park. He arrived on 20 September,[194] in time to see Wallack's National Theatre burn to the ground. One newspaper described Price among other spectators atop the Astor House, "like a fat and well-fed philosopher, detailing what he had done when *his* theatre was on fire." While the National was still burning, he was reported to have made an

[192] *New-Yorker*, 10 November 1838.

[193] Henry Wikoff, *Reminiscences of an Idler* (New York, 1880), pp. 497-501, 514.

[194] *Morning Courier and Inquirer* (New York), 21 September 1839.

overture to Charles Kean, one of Wallack's stars.[195] Wallack transferred his company to a new theatre which had opened the previous season next to Niblo's Garden, but he lost money and had to give it up in mid-November.[196]

Wallack's misfortunes helped the Park, but not so much as might have been expected. Wallack gained considerable sympathy, which generated antagonism to Price, when he declined Simpson's offer of the Park to Wallack's company for a benefit because of the curtness with which it was phrased.[197] Ironically, true-blue Americans championed British-born James Wallack against American-born Stephen Price, presumably corrupted by residence abroad. Fire had removed one competitor, but the Bowery Theatre presented not only melodrama and spectacle but regular tragedy and comedy. Among its stars that season were Edwin Forrest and Charles Kean. The New Chatham took in James and Henry Wallack. It closed in January for financial reasons, but by this time William Mitchell had begun to succeed at the Olympic with a repertory of farce, vaudeville, burletta, and extravaganza. Moreover, the Park, like all the New York theatres, was suffering from the business depression following the financial panic of 1837.

Price pinned his hopes for improvement largely on the coming of Fanny Elssler,[198] but he did not live to see her triumph. This was perhaps as well, for although her engagement made her rich, it further impoverished the Park because of the expense for orchestra and supporting dancers. On 20 January 1840, after a few days' illness, Stephen Price died, probably of erysipelas.[199]

[195] *Morning Herald* (New York), 27 September 1839.

[196] Odell, *Annals*, IV, p. 339.

[197] *Evening Star* (New York), 25 September 1839.

[198] Wikoff, *Reminiscences*, pp. 540-542.

[199] *Times and Courier Intelligencer* (New York), 21 and 28 January 1840.

The death of King Stephen brought sharply different reactions. Macready, a man who never forgave a wrong, real or fancied, noted in his diary: "an arrogant, bullying, envious, and dishonest man. . . . He is gone—unpitied, unlamented: he had no friend."[200] On the other hand, Philip Hone observed: "Poor Price! I could better have spared a better man. I . . . know him to possess many excellent qualities which the world, judging from a rough exterior, and a temper not of the sweetest kind, did not give him credit for. He was a gentleman, but not gentle, a warm, devoted friend, but an unforgiving and implacable enemy, 'open as day to melting charity,' but overbearing and impatient of contradiction."[201]

Stephen Price was in some ways a typical American of his time. He was shrewd in business—sometimes, indeed, less than scrupulous. He acted big and he talked big. Through enterprise and daring he was able to lord it over his fellow managers. The arrogance of the self-made man combined with an irritability, which may well have been caused by his chronic illness, to make King Stephen something of a tyrant.

In one way he was different from the majority of his fellow Americans. A predilection for the English, not surprising in a man whose father had been a Tory during the Revolutionary War, fitted Price well to deal with actors from overseas, and made him content to live in England for thirteen years to supply the Park with talent. Thereby he lost his character as an American. Competitors were able to raise against him the growing anti-British sentiment which culminated nine years later in the bloody Astor Place Riot.

King Stephen reigned in the American theatre for a

---

[200] *Diaries of William Macready*, ed. William Toynbee, 2 vols. (London, 1912), I, p. 45.
[201] 22 January 1840, MS Diary, XVI, NYHS.

quarter-century of its formative years, and he gave direction and impetus to forces which continued long after his death. He did not neglect native-born talent, but his influence was felt in another direction. He was the first to perceive the attraction of star actors from England, and he exploited that attraction with such enterprise that he altered the pattern of theatre operation in this country. When he bought into the management of the Park in 1808, it operated on the basis of a permanent company, augmented occasionally by a visiting star. By the time he left New York for London, the stock company was no longer the backbone of the Park's operation; it existed to support a succession of visiting stars. Other theatres had perforce to follow the Park's example.

In the process of supplying the American stage, Price created a considerable talent drain in England. As manager of Drury Lane, he made no significant innovations. He depended on stars, perhaps even more heavily than Elliston had before him, and like other managers of the day he allowed a successful new piece to run continuously until its popularity was exhausted, instead of putting it into repertory with less attractive offerings. He discovered that the continuous run was uneconomical of acting personnel but took this only as a sign that the stock company was too large.

Either he did not see that the guest star and the continuous run would eventually destroy the stock company or he did not care. He gave audiences what they wanted—what they would pay for. In the reign of King Stephen, it was the box office that ruled.

The Theatrical Management
of Edwin Booth

CHARLES H. SHATTUCK

IN 1863, some three years after Edwin Booth won recognition in New York City as a starring actor, he ventured into theatre management. His motives were in part centered in personal advancement. During the dozen years of his novitiate—stock acting in California and Australia, barnstorming the East in pursuit of stardom, serving under crude commercial managers—he had determined that if he were ever to stand at the head of his profession he must assume governance. His motives were in part liberal: he wished to improve the whole art of theatre in America, and this he could achieve only from a position of control.[1]

From his thirtieth to his fortieth year he was involved in management, and much of his energy during this decade he spent on what appeared finally to be a hopeless cause. He built a splendid theatre, but at absurd expense, struggled desperately through five seasons to pay for it and keep it going, lost it, and fell into bankruptcy. His worst weakness was his business sense. He could not manage affairs of money and he lacked the ability of, say, Henry Irving, to surround himself with loyal and capable officers who could

[1] The principal biographical studies of Booth are: Asia Booth Clarke, *The Elder and Younger Booths* (New York, 1882); William Winter, *Life and Art of Edwin Booth* (New York, 1893; revised, 1894); Edwina Booth Grossmann, *Edwin Booth: recollections by his daughter and letters to her and his friends* (New York, 1894); Richard Lockridge, *Darling of Misfortune* (New York, 1932); Stanley Kimmel, *The Mad Booths of Maryland* (Indianapolis, 1940); Eleanor Ruggles, *Prince of Players* (New York, 1953); Charles H. Shattuck, *The Hamlet of Edwin Booth* (Urbana, 1969).

assist him in such affairs. On the contrary, he made himself easy prey to sharpers. He misjudged the public, too, willfully pursuing his own visions without counting the costs, creating scenic masterpieces which the public could not or would not pay for. The story of his management is a tragedy of idealism unregulated by the facts of life.

Before he built his own theatre he participated in the management of three others, and since all three were financially successful he probably imagined himself much more capable than he really was. Two of these three were purely commercial ventures, which we need not linger over long.

Toward the end of 1863, together with his brother-in-law, the well-known comedian John Sleeper Clarke, he took over the Walnut Street Theatre in Philadelphia, and they operated it in partnership for six and a half years. The idea of this venture originated with Clarke, who did have a sharp eye for business, and Booth joined in as a way of taking his mind off his troubles. It had been the worst year of Booth's life. His wife Mollie had been ill when the year began, and, drowning his worries in brandy, he had nearly ruined himself professionally by acting while drunk. Then Mollie died. The shock of this put an end to his drinking but it left him in a state of morbid depression. He withdrew from the stage and spent the ensuing months in self-lacerating remorse, pouring out his grief and shame in hysterical letters to friends. By the summer's end he had pulled himself together, had established a home in New York where his mother could look after his infant daughter, and was ready for work again. But mere acting wasn't enough. "I feel the need," he wrote to his friend Adam Badeau, "the absolute necessity of something practical—something to draw me out of myself, and if buying theatres on time . . . , furnishing a house &c, &c, won't do me good—nought but a bullet will."[2] The Walnut Street was just the right distraction. It was a "dirty and dingy" place, he explained, but it was *the* theatre of Philadelphia, and the partners expected that merely by filling it with visiting attractions and sometimes playing there themselves they would "make a deal of money out of it."

And so they did. The total price was $100,000, of which they paid down $20,000.[3] A year later, on 5 November 1864, they retired $30,000 of the mortgage. The second year was the frightful one of Lincoln's assassination when Booth, forced into retirement, had little other income than the profits of management, and Clarke too was hard-pressed; yet on 6 October 1865 they paid off $5,000 more. The third year brought a bumper income: on 5 October 1866 they retired the remaining mortgage of $45,000, and the Walnut Street was all their own. The next three and a half seasons netted profits of $75,000, of which Booth's annual share averaged over $10,700. In March of 1870, Booth sold his interest in the Walnut Street to Clarke, so that he could put the capital into his own new theatre in New York City.[4]

Their second commercial venture, though brief, was similarly prosperous. In the summer of 1866 they leased the Boston Theatre for one year only. Booth opened the fall season there with a reconstruction of his Winter Garden *Hamlet* and played it to huge audiences for over three weeks. His whole stand in Boston was so successful that he

---

[2] This and the following sentences are derived from two letters from Booth to Adam Badeau, both dated 26 September, and both apparently written in 1863. One is at The Players and the other at The Folger Shakespeare Library.

[3] The statistics of this paragraph are taken from the "Walnut Street Account Book," The Players.

[4] William Bispham, a financier friend, proposed this transfer of capital in a letter to Booth of 23 January 1868, in The Players.

regretted he had not taken the theatre alone. He could have made more than $30,000 from it, he estimated, besides his share as an actor, "but just like me, I see these chances after they have slipped & gone; as it is I shall make about $8000 at most."[5] As it was, however, he carried off nearly $15,000 (if I read the account books correctly), and had no cause for complaint.[6] Indeed, in the light of other events, I suspect that without Clarke's hand in the partnership, Booth on his own might have muffed it.

It is Booth's involvement in *artistic* management that claims our attention most, of course, and this began at the Winter Garden in the spring of 1864.[7] At that time the partners, feeling the ground firm under them in their first season at the Walnut Street, considered taking a New York theatre where they could establish themselves as permanent metropolitan stars. "Our object," Booth said afterwards, "was solely to elevate the tone of our art, without even 1/2 an eye to the dollar, for we well knew there were not 'millions in it'; no, we would take our chances at making money *outside* of New York & be satisfied with the glory of the good work we would accomplish *there*."

Word floated to them that the lease of the Winter Garden, held these last four years by A. W. "Black Jack" Jackson, was on the market, and that William Stuart, a well-known hanger-on of the New York theatrical scene, was negotiating for it with the owner, Louis La Farge.

---

[5] Booth to John B. Murray, 11 October 1866, The Players.

[6] The "Boston Theatre Account Book" for this 1866-67 season is at The Players.

[7] The following account of the Booth-Clarke relationship with William Stuart, including all quotations not otherwise identified, is largely derived from a 14-page letter from Booth to Harry Magonigle, 14 November 1874, in which Booth sets down "all that I can recall of my connections with Stuart," The Folger Shakespeare Library. Booth's attitude toward Stuart is unreservedly, but at most points deservedly, hostile.

Booth and Clarke discussed their "grand air castle" with Stuart, and that "foxy old adventurer" (so Booth calls him) encouraged them to join him. He assured them that they would be the artists of the establishment, bringing honor to the profession, and that he would not only relieve them of all business cares but through his connections with the press he would be their "Hazlitt," too, to analyze, criticize, and celebrate their work in disinterested and penetrating reviews.

This sounds improbable. It *was* improbable. To understand what would follow we must take a reckoning of William Stuart. He was not the first rascal with whom Booth naively got entangled during his career, nor would he be the last, but he was one of the worst.

Stuart was born in Ireland in 1821, and his real name was Edmund O'Flaherty.[8] In the early 1850's, as a member of a London fast set, he got into trouble over racing debts (or some say a political indiscretion); in 1853 he fled to America and changed his name to Stuart. In March of 1855, being employed on the New York *Tribune*, he turned theatre critic and perpetrated a series of outrageous attacks upon the acting of Edwin Forrest.[9] This was how he came to consider himself a "Hazlitt."

Next he turned theatre manager. For two seasons he controlled Wallack's. In 1859-60 he was the partner of Dion Boucicault when they refurbished the Metropolitan, dressed it with hanging baskets of perfumed paper flowers, and dubbed it the Winter Garden.[10] For the next four seasons,

[8] On Stuart's career and character, see also Winter, *Life and Art*, pp. 114-120, and Daniel J. Watermeier, *Between Actor and Critic* (Princeton, 1971), p. 19. Stuart died on 26 December 1886.

[9] The *Tribune* (New York), 20 March to 3 April 1855.

[10] G.C.D. Odell, *Annals of the New York Stage* (New York, 1927-49), VII, p. 210; Joseph Jefferson, *The Autobiography* (New York, 1897), pp. 207-208.

during "Black Jack" Jackson's management of the Winter Garden, Stuart remained there in some unknowable capacity. He would claim in after years that it was he who held the lease, and that he only permitted Jackson to govern it on his behalf.[11] Booth, who acted under Jackson, remembered it otherwise. Stuart was the most servile of underlings, Booth tells us, "always hat in hand in Jackson's presence"; Jackson treated him "worse than a decent man would treat a mangy cur," once told him to "take a *back seat* when *honesty* was talked of," once, indeed, charged him with robbing the box office and cursed him to his heart's content.

When Stuart was in money, he could be a gay, affectionate, amusing man, a *bon vivant* and charming conversationalist who entertained friends lavishly at clubs and at his country place near New London. The epithet "dear boy" was so often on his lips that "Dear Boy Stuart" was his common nickname. Booth was apparently taken in by his affability at the beginning of their professional association and spent considerable time in his company. But Stuart was vain, spiteful, and unscrupulous, an inveterate self-seeker and double-dealer who would sacrifice anyone to a rally of wit. He would praise Booth to his face and then ridicule him behind his back (especially to newspaper friends) as conceited, difficult, and "Hamlet-y." According to William Winter, "All the stock misrepresentations of Booth that have drifted through the American press originated with him."[12] He would claim that he had "made" Booth's reputation, that without his promotion Booth would have been nobody.[13]

[11] This and other of Stuart's false claims to proprietorship of the Winter Garden appear in the *Spirit of the Times*, 30 March 1867, at the time of the Winter Garden fire.

[12] Winter, *Life and Art*, p. 119.

[13] Stuart's opinions of Booth which follow here were reported soon after Booth's death in 1893 by a journalist named Joe Howard. For Howard, see the *Dramatic Mirror* (New York), 11 April 1908. "How-

Booth was lazy. Booth was stingy. Booth was jealous of competition and surrounded himself with wooden actors the better to show off his own limited talent. Stuart made it all seem a wry joke. As for Booth's reputation as an "intellectual" actor, Stuart dismissed that with a cheerful sneer: "During the many weeks he has passed at my cottage I have never seen him read a book—hardly a newspaper. He has sat the livelong day in a cloud of smoke, revolving the great question whether Desdemona's bed should be on the side or in the centre of the stage." Booth's supposed veneration of Shakespeare only reminded Stuart of that mayor of Stratford-on-Avon who once declared, "I do not know much about Shakespeare, but I believe in keeping him up for the good of the town."

One of Stuart's crooked claims in later years was that after 1864 (as before) *he* was sole manager of the Winter Garden, and that at considerable loss to himself he permitted Booth to do whatever he pleased in the artistic way. Now, it happened that Booth and Clarke were in the room (though not intending to share in the negotiations) on the day when Stuart and his lawyer met with La Farge to sign the lease. There was disagreement. Finally La Farge crossed the room to the actors and said, "Boys, are you going to help old Stuart to manage this thing? *He* says so, & if it is so, why *all right*—but otherwise he can't have it." At the end of the session, it appears, all three men signed the lease, and Booth and Clarke somewhat unexpectedly found themselves co-managers of their favorite New York theatre.

If Stuart felt balked at not getting sole possession he did not show it. One foot in the door was enough for the pres-

ard's Letter: Stories about Booth from Stuart, his Old Manager," a clipping in The Harvard Theatre Collection.

ent. His next ploy was to draw up a tripartite agreement for sharing responsibilities and expenses. It was incredibly brazen. He, Stuart, was to control everything. They, Booth and Clarke, were to pay the whole rent, and their financial take was to be only a portion of the profit only on the nights when they acted. Not even Booth, surely, would have signed such an agreement, but it devolved upon Clarke to draw up the appropriate counterproposal: the actors took half the profits, after expenses, on their own nights; Stuart received a weekly salary of seventy dollars for serving as "front man" and taking care of all affairs before the curtain; the three shared equally in the overall profits of the season. Stuart, balked again, "pretended to be delighted, & overpowered by gratitude, & assured us . . . it was far more to his advantage than the plan he had offered."

The terms agreed upon, they set to work. Or rather, Booth insists, *he* set to work. He alone took charge of renovating the auditorium, which under "Black Jack" had degenerated badly. When the theatre opened in mid-August, the *Spirit of the Times* printed a description of its new aspect which gives us a clear notion of what Booth's labor had been:

> All is fresh, clean, and *couleur de rose* from the external iron gates to the back of the stage. The dust-heaps have been cleared out—the ragged old matting, over which you were continually tripping yourself up, replaced by new—enough light admitted to enable you to see where you are going to, who is your next door neighbor, and whether it is Brown or Smith that walks on the stage . . . which is now furnished with one of the new and improved sunk "flotes," instead of the old-style row of raised burners, with reflectors so unsightly, and so provoking when you were desirous of ascertaining whether a lady

had a pretty foot or not. The whole of the auditorium has been repainted and redecorated. Boucicault's dirty old flower-baskets, and dirtier bunches of artificial flowers, have been removed from their time-honored position, and replaced by well-executed fresco panels; the upper tier, proscenium, and, in fact, every portion of the front of the house equally displays the liberality and good taste of the new management—the *ensemble* being light, elegant, and cheerful.[14]

The public doubtless credited the smiling Stuart with these improvements, but Booth claims that his partners were "doing and knowing very little about the matter," that the work was all his own.[15]

But an issue far weightier than good housekeeping now engaged him. Now, he knew, was the precise moment in his career when he must transform himself from mere actor into actor-manager in the grand tradition. He had been reading John Doran's *Annals of the Stage* and identifying himself with Doran's idealized portraits of "Their Majesties' Servants," especially Thomas Betterton: "He is my ideal of an actor, both on and off the stage. He aimed at truth in art, and lived it at home. I wish he lived today, or that I had lived then."[16] It was his wish, he wrote to Emma Cary, "to bring out several of the Shaksperian plays in a superior style, and the whole management is in my hands. I've been in the scene-room and wardrobe night and day, lately."[17] The first of these revivals would be *Hamlet*, of course, and

14 *Spirit of the Times*, 27 August 1864.

15 Booth to Mrs. Richard Cary, 12 July 1864, printed in Grossmann, *Edwin Booth*, p. 160.

16 Booth to Emma Cary, 11 November [1864], printed in Grossmann, *Edwin Booth*, p. 155.

17 Booth to Emma Cary, 26 August 1864, printed in Grossmann, *Edwin Booth*, p. 164.

for the first time in America it would be staged worthily. He hired a skilled scene painter, John Thorne, to prepare the exterior scenes, and a brilliant young newcomer, Charles Witham, to do the seven or eight interiors. Together they would create an authentic vision of the tenth century court at Elsinore. "Every scene, every dress, every chair & table— and nearly all the actors will be new," he wrote to Adam Badeau. "Some of the pictures in the play will be what has never been used on any stage in America & I doubt if Kean did anything like it."[18]

On top of all else came a call from the Shakespeare Centenary Committee, which was raising funds to erect a Shakespeare statue in Central Park. Booth undertook to get up a benefit performance of *Julius Caesar* in which "The Three Sons of the Great Booth"—himself, Junius Brutus Junior, and John Wilkes—would share the leads.[19] This should have taken place in early July, but the vagaries of John Wilkes—off somewhere supposedly attending to his "oil business" but more probably fomenting political conspiracy—delayed the event to the last possible moment. The *Caesar* performance finally occurred on 25 November, the night before the opening of *Hamlet*.

It had been a killing summer. By September, when Booth went down to Philadelphia to do his stint at the Walnut Street Theatre, he was exhausted: "Never since I began my theatrical career did its labors seem so truly to resemble downright bodily, mental, and spiritual 'hammer and tongs' as now. . . . For the past year I have realized the hateful truth that the human, or, rather, the mortal, part of me, is

[18] Booth to Adam Badeau, 14 October 1864, The Folger Shakespeare Library.

[19] References to the coming on of the *Caesar* production appear in Booth's letters to Emma Cary, 17 June and 11 November, 1864, printed in Grossmann, *Edwin Booth*, pp. 153, 154.

not equal to its duties."[20] By mid-October he was for a while actually ill, "confined to the house, and obliged to sit upright, with my leg in a sling; my old enemy, the neuralgia, has made me quite lame and disagreeable."[21] Yet illness from overwork was better than despondency. He had found in his métier "something practical—something to draw me out of myself."

So far as I know, Booth never set down any formal statement of the managerial principles by which he conducted his work at the Winter Garden, or at Booth's Theatre afterwards. It would hardly have been in character for him to do so. Yet by a search backward into earlier events, a search into his correspondences, a search into the events of his eight producing seasons, we can extract those principles which most clearly activated him.

To begin with, we must reckon with the motive of professional pride. By this I do not mean personal vanity, but simple awareness of his own status as a theatre artist. Augustin Daly came to theatre management as a playwright, his first concern being always to draw an ensemble toward the best possible execution of the *play*. Jarrett and Palmer came to management essentially as promoters and business men, their first concern being to produce whatever would lure the best-paying audiences to the box office. But Booth was above all an actor, and a starring actor at that. Born into the star system, he had earned the position of "A-number-1," and having achieved such eminence it would have been suicidal to abandon it. When he turned manager, he was *actor*-manager, in the tradition of Garrick and Kemble, Macready and Charles Kean—the leading performer in

[20] Booth to Mrs. Richard Cary, 16 September [1864], printed in Grossmann, *Edwin Booth*, p. 161.

[21] Booth to Emma Cary, 15 October 1864, printed in Grossmann, *Edwin Booth*, p. 164.

his own establishment. The public would not have had it otherwise.

He was by no means greedy of place nor jealous of the abilities of others. When he built Booth's Theatre he honestly intended it to be a showplace for every great actor of the day, though for the most part this intention was baffled. He wanted Edwin Forrest to open Booth's Theatre in *Othello*, but Forrest rebuffed every approach. He sought repeatedly to engage Charles Fechter, but Fechter declined his invitations.[22] Joe Jefferson did come more than once, to Booth's considerable profit. Charlotte Cushman came too and shed honor on the house, but the salary she demanded was a luxury Booth could not often afford. He was eager to promote younger or lesser artists—Ned Adams, Theodore Hamilton, Lawrence Barrett—by giving them star billing in their own plays, but the public turned away. "I think it is definitely proved that the draught to my house lies in *my* name," he once had to tell the importunate Barrett; and again, desperately, "I cannot afford to *star* those who have proved unprofitable to me."[23]

The company of his theatre never became the first-rate and stable ensemble that he wished to build, but, in the nature of things, was a mere stock company working in support of stars, its membership always changing. Try as he might to secure the best talent and train them and keep them, few actors of real worth could submit to his salary

[22] Barton Hill's efforts to bring Forrest to Booth's Theatre are reported in his "Personal Recollections of Edwin Booth," which appeared in the *Dramatic Mirror* (New York), 26 December 1896. In a letter of 13 June 1867 now at The Players, Booth asked Lawrence Barrett, then in London, to urge Fechter to delay his New York visit until Booth's Theatre would be ready to receive him. A letter from Fechter to Booth excusing himself from a later invitation is in Booth's souvenir letter-book at The Players.

[23] Booth to Lawrence Barrett, 29 November 1871 and 26 December 1872, The Players.

schedule or to the artistic subservience which the star system imposed upon them. Ned Adams, for instance, admitted that his year as Booth's leading man was worth $20,000 to him elsewhere,[24] but he had to go elsewhere to get it. Theodore Hamilton and Fanny Morant detached themselves for more profitable employment after a season or so. Only the inept, the humdrum, and the superannuated wanted to stay on. Thus in many ways Booth's own eminence and the star system which he inevitably perpetuated undermined the success of his enterprise.

Although we cannot tolerate William Stuart's sneering belittlement of Booth's "intellect," it is the sneer that offends us more than the kernel of his charge. No one would give Booth high marks as an "intellectual." Adam Badeau, who knew him far more intimately than Stuart ever could and had better brains to understand him, once described him as "a man strangely constituted, of exquisite susceptibilities. . . . His mind is not trained in any logical fashion; he is a man of genius, of perceptions and emotions, and cannot reason."[25] This does not mean, however, that Booth was not amenable to intellectual influences. In the 1850's, under Badeau's guidance, the encouragement of his fiancée Mollie Devlin, and his associations with painters and sculptors, he had absorbed a good deal of common culture, literary and artistic.[26] By this means he had restyled his acting— cleansed it of frontier roughness and deepened its suggestive power—so that it appealed to the "best" elements of the theatre-going public. "Art" became his watchword, and he hungered after a wider artistic experience than America could afford him. Early in 1860, even before he had won a

[24] Booth to Lawrence Barrett, 20 November 1870, The Players.

[25] Badeau to James Harrison Wilson, 12 September 1863, Princeton University Library, Special Collections.

[26] Shattuck, *The Hamlet of Edwin Booth*, pp. 18-36.

place in the New York theatre, he wrote his friend Richard Cary that he was soon going abroad, "but whether for Italy, France, or 'Merrie England' depends upon—away, away from here at all events. Art degenerates below the standard even of a trade in America. My taste is becoming vitiated; my love of it is dying out; and I need the recuperation. . . . I daresay I shall have ample opportunities to study art in its native atmosphere, and to inhale enough of the latter to vivify my future productions with something of the true and the beautiful."[27] Mollie Devlin had been urging him to this. "The society of Artists in all countries but our own," she wrote him, "is said to be more charming than of all other classes—for art, with all save us, is religion. We shall see this when we go abroad. 'Twill encourage and assist you, darling, in the mission you are to perform toward your sinking art here."[28]

Notice Booth's reference to "the true and the beautiful," and Mollie's assertion that "art is religion." She had been reading, and making Booth read, the philosophical discourses of Victor Cousin, *The True, the Beautiful, and the Good*, that most lucid summation of philosophical idealism. And Booth aspired to realize in his acting, as Cousin told him Phidias and Michelangelo and Raphael had realized in the plastic arts, that religion of beauty which elevates the soul toward the infinite, up the pathway to God.[29]

When he did visit Europe a year later, his studies of "art," I fear, did not go very deep. He never got to Italy. English art did not interest him. Turner's late work, which,

[27] Booth to Richard Cary, 1860, printed in Grossmann, *Edwin Booth*, p. 132.

[28] Mollie Devlin to Booth, 10 May 1860, Theatre Collection of the New York Public Library.

[29] Shattuck, *The Hamlet of Edwin Booth*, pp. 33-34.

after Ruskin, everyone was talking about, seemed to him "all bosh and whitewash."[30] If at the Louvre he found God's plenty of historical paintings and Renaissance masterpieces, his interest there took a predictably utilitarian direction: "I've been studying costumes all day at the Louvre," he wrote Badeau. "I've got old Richelieu to a dot."[31]

The point is that as an intellectual Booth was by no means progressive, inventive, forward-looking. Art for him was Raphael, drama was Shakespeare (or Bulwer or Hugo, Shakespeare's modern imitators), criticism stopped with Goethe and Hazlitt, esthetics came to rest in Cousin. Isolated by circumstance, faith, and temperament from every fresh creative stir in the world, whether in literature or science, politics or art, he was intellectually a conservative, solely allegiant to the art and ideas of the past.

In the English theatre, where he acted for a few months in 1861, his conservative instincts were confirmed. London still basked in the afterglow of Charles Kean's recently concluded management at the Princess's. For nine years fashionable audiences had delighted in Kean's gorgeous historicized productions of Shakespeare, and the record of Kean's work had already been immortalized in J. W. Cole's encyclopedic *Life and Theatrical Times of Charles Kean*. From that book Booth could take lessons and inspiration. If Kean, whose personal talent was less than remarkable, could attract the most discriminating playgoers of London with the arts of stage production, why could not Booth do the same in New York? He might restore to health the depraved Gothamite taste for melodrama, farce, minstrelsy, variety shows, French sensation drama, and the likes of

[30] Booth to Adam Badeau, 8 April 1862, The Folger Shakespeare Library. See also Booth to Thomas Hicks, 9 December 1861, Theatre Collection of the New York Public Library.
[31] Booth to Adam Badeau, 8 April 1862.

Adah Isaacs Menken. This was what Mollie meant by his "mission toward his sinking art": "To see an Art as *holy* as the drama so desecrated and perverted—is it not outrageous?" she had said. "How glad I am, dear one, that the branch you were fitted for has not been degraded, for though unappreciated now—the day will come when 'gorgeous Tragedy' will have its sway! You are held as its only true representative in this day—and you can, if you will, change the perverted taste of the public, by your truth and sublimity."[32]

There were two principles to capitalize on, two slogans by which Shakespeare and "gorgeous Tragedy" could be brought into fresh estate. They were "fit illustration" and "restoration of the true text." By these William Charles Macready had long since won great reputation in his brief stands at Covent Garden and Drury Lane; and after him Kean had triumphantly advanced the more visible and fetching of these—scenic splendor grounded in historical accuracy. Witness the ringing tribute paid to Kean by the Duke of Newcastle at Kean's farewell dinner:

> His sceneries are not only lessons in art, but they are lessons in history. (Hear, hear.) We have become, of late years, many of us, attached to archaeology. I look upon Mr. Kean as one of the greatest archaeologists of the day. (Hear, hear.) He has had a reason for everything; there is nothing which he introduces upon the stage for which he has not authority, and you may see living representations of Shakespeare's characters, with the exact costume, the exact scenery, the exact furniture of the rooms which . . . existed at the time Shakespeare represented.[33]

[32] Mollie Devlin to Booth, 24 January 1860, Theatre Collection of the New York Public Library.

[33] J. W. Cole, *Life and Theatrical Times of Charles Kean* (London, 1859), II, p. 366.

Kean himself, addressing his last audience at the Princess's, had devoted more than half of his long farewell address to a defense and celebration of his achievement in "historical accuracy."[34]

Booth could not improve upon Kean's archaeologism, but he could emulate it. And, on the other hand, he could surpass Kean as a "restorer." "Now I (egotist!)," he wrote Emma Cary as the time approached for the opening of Booth's Theatre, "intend to go even beyond Chas. Kean in my devotion to the sacred text of the late W.S. I intend restoring to the stage (to mine, at least) the unadulterated plays of Shakspere: his 'Romeo and Juliet', not so performed since the days of Betterton, I fancy . . . ; 'Richard III', which Chas. Kean feared to attempt, and offered a weak apology for retaining the Cibber version. . . . I pity his feeble correction of Shakspere's geographical blunders in 'Winter's Tale'. He should have ascertained the name of the town in which the wise man lived who jumped into a brier-bush."[35]

This is not a formal statement, of course, but only an off-hand playful bluster in a letter to a friend. It is not accurate, either about the past or about what is to come. Booth seems not to have known that Charlotte Cushman "restored" *Romeo and Juliet* some twenty-five years earlier.[36] He would not restore the Shakespearean *Richard III* at his own theatre, but only repeat Cibber's version. Except for returning to Shakespeare's fanciful geography in *The Winter's Tale* he mainly abided by Kean's arrangement of that play.[37] His "devotion to the sacred text" was as cooled

[34] Cole, *Charles Kean*, II, pp. 378-385.

[35] Booth to Emma Cary, 27 September 1868, printed in Grossmann, *Edwin Booth*, p. 176.

[36] At the Haymarket in London on 29 December 1845. See G.C.D. Odell, *Shakespeare from Betterton to Irving* (New York, 1920), II, 271-272.

[37] Booth to Henry Hinton, 26 April [1868], The Folger Shakespeare Library.

down by personal taste and temporal circumstance as that of Macready or any other of the nineteenth-century restorers. He cut from the texts all apparent bawdry and impiety, all seeming obscurity and redundancy, and much else that was dispensable to a rapid-running drama focusing on the central action and the central characters. It can be acknowledged only that he did study the texts conscientiously and that his better stage versions, however lopped and bowdlerized, were the product of his own careful, if limited, thinking.

One managerial responsibility he could not rise to was the cultivation and encouragement of new drama. In earlier days Mollie had urged him to do so. For all her devotion to "gorgeous Tragedy," she foresaw that he must be more than a curator of traditional values. "You know the day for the stately and grand is passed," she wrote. "Vary your repertory by things more suitable to the present age; people live in the Future now, not in the Past."[38] Warnings on this matter came later from other directions. When he opened Booth's Theatre with *Romeo and Juliet,* a writer in the *Spirit of the Times* pointed out that Shakespeare alone would not sustain his "splendid enterprise." If the house was crowded nightly it was not on Shakespeare's account. The real attractions were, first, the novelty of the new theatre; second, the beauty of the scenery; third, Booth himself: the drawing power of Shakespeare was a bad fourth.[39] After his 1870 *Hamlet,* the critic Nym Crinkle warned him that what modern audiences really wanted was the flesh-and-blood reality of drama like Tom Taylor's *Mary Warner,* where one is "out of the pedantry and priggishness of *technique* at once into the warm atmosphere of expectation, with a human interest glowing in all faces, and every man,

[38] Mollie Devlin to Booth, 28 December 1859, The Players.
[39] *Spirit of the Times,* 20 February 1869.

woman, and child content to leave his or her foot-rule and scales at home, and for an hour or two give themselves up to an illusion which looks like life."[40]

Booth had, in fact, produced *Mary Warner* with Kate Bateman a few months earlier, and Miss Bateman's passionate agony in the title-role had indeed drawn well at the box office; but no one who now reads that play can take Nym Crinkle's argument very seriously or blame Booth much for declining to build a program upon such naive stuff. Shakespeare came first with him, and there was so little time. Occasionally he brought out other new plays for other actors—*Enoch Arden* for Ned Adams, *The Man o' Airlie* for Lawrence Barrett—but after *The Fool's Revenge*, which he introduced to New York as early as 1864, he added nothing modern to his own repertory. The main thrust of his management was not to advance the new drama, but to preserve the old: through the arts of acting and production to protect, in museum fashion, the classics of the past.

To RETURN TO the 1864 opening of the Winter Garden: The pattern for the season, the pattern which Booth would adopt thereafter as his standard, was as follows: beginning in mid-August, Clarke would play one hundred nights of comedy; toward the end of the year Booth would come in for one hundred nights of heavy drama; the final three months or so would be filled by visiting stars.[41]

Hamlet, which opened on 26 November, was supposed to play for only a month. Booth intended it to be the first in a *series* of great plays "framed appropriately." But success spoiled his intentions. *Hamlet* caught on. It ran and ran, until Booth was "heartily sick & wearied of the monotonous

---

40 The *World* (New York), 16 January 1870.

41 For the Winter Garden repertory, 1864-67, see G.C.D. Odell, *Annals of the New York Stage*, VII, pp. 637-643; VIII, pp. 17-22, 145-151.

work." He grew stale and repeatedly suggested a change of bill. But Stuart, caring for nothing more than notoriety, would exclaim, "No, not at all, my dear boy! Keep it up— keep it up! If it goes for a year, keep it up."[42] And so they kept it up until 22 March, when it passed into history as the "Hundred Nights Hamlet." In after years Booth would wryly insist that the medal presented to him in commemoration of the event ought really to have been given to Stuart, who by dint of puffery, papering the house, and cajolery had created the sensational run. It was, however, a landmark in Booth's career, an advertisement which he long profited from. For once, at least, Stuart was justified in claiming that he had "made" Booth's reputation.

Three weeks later, on 14 April, Booth having completed his Winter Garden engagement and gone to Boston, the nation was stunned by the assassination of President Lincoln. All theatres were closed during the two-week period of national mourning, but thereafter the Winter Garden ran on according to plan. The old comedian Henry Placide came in for five weeks, then Barton Hill for two weeks in a play of Tom Taylor's, and the season closed with six weeks of a tragedienne from the provinces named Jean Hosmer.

The second season repeated the pattern of the first. From 6 September 1865 to the end of December, Clarke, with a three-week assist by John Brougham, filled the time with comedy, farce, and melodrama. Although after the assassination it had been doubtful that Booth would ever act again, on 3 January 1866 he returned in *Hamlet*, cheered wildly by a crowded house. A month later he brought out his second and equally splendid revival—Bulwer's *Richelieu*. This ran for forty-two nights and with a scattering of

[42] Booth to Harry Magonigle, 14 November 1874, quoted in Winter, *Life and Art*, p. 78.

other roles it carried him through his scheduled three months. April and May brought the Irish fun of Mr. and Mrs. Barney Williams.[43]

During this second season Booth and Clarke were again alerted to William Stuart's devious ways.[44] They discovered that when the lease had come up for renewal Stuart had surreptitiously, by worming his way into the confidence of the agent of La Farge's widow (Louis La Farge had died), acquired the lease for himself alone. They further found that he had been lending this agent money out of the theatre's treasury at a stiff interest rate and was pocketing the profits. Alarmed by the possibility of even worse fiddling, Booth installed his friend Harry Magonigle to keep an eye on the books. Stuart took umbrage at this and (so Booth believed) heightened his campaign of vilifying Booth to his newspaper friends. At the end of the season the sensible Clarke withdrew from the partnership; but Booth, careless of everything but glory, paid Clarke $10,000 for his share of the property and plunged ahead.[45]

Without Clarke's assistance the third season's program at the Winter Garden had to be altered somewhat, and Booth, who was now involved in three enterprises (the Walnut Street, the Boston, and the Winter Garden), had to contribute more effort. While he was opening the Boston sea-

[43] During 1866, as an adjunct to his program of management Booth encouraged the actor Henry Hinton to edit and publish his acting versions. The first three to appear were *Hamlet*, 1866; *Richelieu*, 1867; *The Merchant of Venice*, 1867. At least eight other plays followed, but Booth was dissatisfied with Hinton's work, and in 1876 he commissioned William Winter to replace them with the promptbook edition. Booth's letters to Hinton are preserved at The Folger Shakespeare Library.

[44] The following details are from Booth's letter to Harry Magonigle, 14 November 1874.

[45] Booth to J. H. McVicker, 18 February 1876, The Folger Shakespeare Library.

son with *Hamlet*, the Winter Garden displayed a couple of "she-stars": a week of Jean Davenport Lander in *Adrienne Lecouvreur* and five weeks of Mrs. D. P. Bowers in *Lady Audley's Secret, East Lynne, Donna Diana*, and as her epicene Romeo. In December the Maretzek Opera Company came in, but to play only three nights a week: Booth had to fill the alternate nights with *Hamlet, Richelieu*, and other items. At the end of December he was host to a macaronic *Othello*, with Bogumil Dawison playing Othello in German, Booth Iago in English, and Madame Methua-Scheller speaking Desdemona in whichever language befitted the partner of her scenes.

When in January Booth took the stage for himself he intended by a massive effort to occupy it to the end of the season. For three weeks he offered stock productions of seven of his standard roles. On 28 January he presented his third grand classical revival, *The Merchant of Venice*. His own Shylock—a role he could never really master—was held to be too coarse and ranting, but Charles Witham's scenery, based on Venetian sketches by Emanuel Leutze, was sufficiently beautiful to keep *The Merchant* going for eight weeks. Meanwhile he readied a fourth grand revival, *Romeo and Juliet*. But on the morning of 23 March the Winter Garden was destroyed by fire.

Booth is said to have lost $40,000 that morning,[46] besides the three years' labor that had gone into the scenery and dresses of four productions. But it set him free of William Stuart. As Joe Jefferson put it, "If you had lost a dozen theatres, & as many wardrobes, it would be a cheap release from him."[47] All to be feared from Stuart now was his lies, and Booth put his friends on guard. "Stuart is black at the core," he wrote to his artist friend Jervis McEntee, "and will kill

[46] Lockridge, *Darling of Misfortune*, p. 175.
[47] Booth to John B. Murray, 13 June 1867, The Players.

himself in time, but he can spit venom yet, & should be fanged."[48] He asked McEntee to alert William Winter to the facts of the case, for Winter, he said, was one of the few members of the *corps dramatique* whom he respected and wanted to win to his cause. This was shrewd. In William Winter he would soon find the "Hazlitt" (I use the metaphor with reservations) whose aid he had long been seeking.

THE FIRE SET Booth free also to realize an idea he had been nursing for some months: he would build a theatre of his own.[49] Friends from all sides encouraged him to do so. His reputation as both actor and producer clearly warranted it. But there were obstacles. Desirable locations were few, and once the owners of such property got wind of Booth's intentions prices skyrocketed. And none of Booth's friends who cheered him on were willing or able to back him with money. His brother Junius and Orlando Tompkins of the Boston Theatre wanted to come in with him, but he found their terms preposterous. The wily Stuart offered a list of "speculative pals," which of course he rejected. So he began to reckon what he could raise from a starring tour, and decided to proceed alone.

Then one April day in Boston, with no shrewd Clarke or honest Magonigle on hand to advise him, he walked straight into a trap. Richard A. Robertson, the Boston manager of the mercantile firm of Treadwell and Company, was a very

[48] Booth to Jervis McEntee, 21 November 1867, The Players.

[49] In January he had told John Murray that if he had the money he would build a theatre at Twenty-third Street and Fourth Avenue— Booth to John B. Murray, 15 January 1867, The Players. The following account of the building of Booth's Theatre and Booth's relations with Richard Robertson is mainly derived from an 18-page record which Booth compiled for J. H. McVicker on 18 February 1876, in The Folger Shakespeare Library. Throughout this document Booth blames his own folly, but his attitude toward Robertson is extremely hostile. In matters of detail he was not always accurate.

dear friend of many years' standing. Booth stopped at Robertson's office to chat about his "monomania" and his difficulty in getting a financial starter. To his surprise and delight Robertson said that *he* could help, that he would be proud to associate with Booth in such an enterprise, that (selfishly, he said) he saw a "big thing" in it for himself. After some quick pencilling he declared that the whole cost of land, building, scenery, and dresses ought not to exceed half a million. What if they had $300,000 to begin with? He could raise half that amount at once: $75,000 by the sale of his tack factory at Taunton, the other $75,000 on credit through Treadwell and Company. Booth could easily bring in $150,000 from a season on the road. Of course they could swing it. The thing was as good as done. Now on what terms should they divide the profits?

Booth proposed share and share alike. Robertson objected, generously enough, that Booth's share should be the greater, since Booth's name added weight to his half of the investment. They agreed then that Booth should take four-sevenths and Robertson three-sevenths of the profits. They further agreed, since Booth insisted that ultimately the property must belong to him alone, that the property should stand in Booth's name and at the end of five years (or sooner if he wished to) Booth could buy Robertson out. When that event occurred Robertson would presumably have won back his $150,000. If not, Booth would make up the difference, and furthermore Booth would pay Robertson a $100,000 bonus, that sum being calculated as interest on the loan and compensation to Robertson for overseeing the construction of the theatre and managing its affairs while Booth was on the road.

Dazzled by Robertson's generosity and manifest skill with figures and knowing nothing at this time of Robertson's reputation for shady deals "on the street," Booth agreed to everything. He could not foresee that Robertson would never put a penny of real money into the venture, would never even sell his tack factory, but would only cash paper and kite loans which in the long run Booth would have to make good.

Back in New York, Harry Magonigle and an associate named Delafield explored for real estate. The southeast corner of Twenty-third Street and Sixth Avenue, though somewhat removed from Broadway and ridiculously expensive, was the best that they could find. Booth, infected with Robertsonian optimism, insisted that he must *"buy* and *own* the land & not be bothered with leases, rents, &c." He plunged. On 29 May he bought from I. A. Page a parcel of seven lots, giving him a Twenty-third Street frontage of 164 feet and a Sixth Avenue frontage of 60 feet.[50] This much cost $165,000. It was not enough. On 10 July he bought one more 25-foot lot (Dr. Peckham's) on Twenty-third Street, raising that frontage to 189 feet. At $2000 per front foot, that scrap of ground cost him $50,000. In September he put out $35,500 more, buying and trading lots on Sixth Avenue to extend that frontage to 79 feet. Thus the total cost of the ground alone came to $250,500, over half the sum which Robertson had proposed to cover the whole venture. Booth paid down $90,500 in cash and incurred interest charges of $10,000 a year on the mortgaged remainder. In this wild flinging about of money and paper, the mere $1216.25 paid to the lawyer, Bruorton, for searching titles was hardly noticeable. For, as Booth sourly reflected years afterward,

[50] The financial figures which follow are derived from the "Booth's Theatre Account Books," The Players, and from a letter from Harry Magonigle to J. H. McVicker, 9 February 1876, in The Folger Shakespeare Library. A ground plan of the lots purchased has been constructed by Gerald Honaker in "Edwin Booth, Producer" (unpublished dissertation, Indiana University, 1969), p. 95.

"We were rich. We owned a tack factory and a popular actor."

In the search for an architect Booth let Delafield persuade him to take on the firm of Renwick and Sands (relatives of Delafield's), a decision which he later declared "fatal," for they were "incapable of such a work." At this point Robertson intruded his brother John into the arrangements. John Robertson owned a sawmill in Boston, could therefore get lumber cheaply, and must therefore (if logic collapses here, Booth seems not to have noticed) be installed as superintendent of the builders.

About 1 June, leaving the Robertsons in charge of the architects and his not very intelligent brother Joseph Booth in charge of the account books, Booth went west to gather dollars. And there at once an unexpectable complication arose: love. As Booth explained it afterwards, "A new life began to dawn upon me in the midst of these distracting and displeasing business matters, & my mind was far too busy with the future to feel much interest in the present. . . . I let things go . . . and gave myself up entirely to the contemplation of what was to be of greater import, & far more *real* than theatre, or acting or fame or dollars."[51] The girl was Mary McVicker, stepdaughter of the Chicago theatre manager James McVicker. In early June she played Juliet to his Romeo. A few days later he was writing to friends in New York that she would be the opening attraction at his theatre, and that "she will be the best actress we've had for a century in this country."[52] For the next year and a half she toured with him as his leading lady, and as often as possible

[51] Booth to J. H. McVicker, 18 February 1876, quoted in Winter, *Life and Art*, p. 91.

[52] Booth to Launt Thompson, 9 June [1867], Theatre Collection of the New York Public Library; Booth to John B. Murray, 13 June 1867, The Players. For an objective account of Mary McVicker, see Winter, *Life and Art*, pp. 91-95.

he featured her as Juliet. Infatuation quite unhinged his judgment. She was in fact a very second-rate actress—tiny, fretful, hard-voiced, aggressive—and doomed to failure on the New York stage. Booth's marriage to her was a sorry mismatch of personalities which ended a dozen years later in her insanity and early death.

The building progressed with agonizing slowness. Scheduled to open in September of 1868, it was not ready until February 1869, half its first season lost. Weeks had been sacrificed at the beginning because the excavation had to be made through solid rock. More loss of time may be blamed on the incompetence of the architects and the inefficiencies of John Robertson; more still upon Booth's extravagant plans for interior decoration. And the technical crews let Booth down. The scene painters, Charles Witham and Henry Hilliard, in over a year's work had finished only thirty scenes. "Do you not consider it a d—dnable affair?" Booth complained to Robertson.[53] They would have to bring in stock scenes from the Walnut Street Theatre to piece out their productions, and at this rate they could not count on more than one grand revival per season. Smith Tuthill ("the half-witted carpenter," Booth called him) had built the under-stage hoisting devices for scene change but could not make them work. Booth was frantic—"bewildered and disgusted with the impracticability of many of his idiotic and extravagant mechanical contrivances." They did not all work on the opening night, and in his welcoming address Booth had to warn the audience of the "bungling" they were about to witness.[54]

The building which emerged twenty months after the

[53] Booth to Richard Robertson [16 November 1868], The Folger Shakespeare Library.

[54] The *World* (New York), 4 February 1869. A quite different version of Booth's opening address is given in Winter, *Life and Art*, pp. 96-97.

first purchase of ground was really two buildings. Fronting on Sixth Avenue was a five-story office structure, with a domestic apartment, which was to be Booth's home, at the top. Booth had hoped to create in this building a sort of arts colony, the space to be let as studios to his numerous artist friends, but, many of them being abroad at the time and others shying off for reasons of expense, the space was largely taken by commercial enterprises.[55] The income from rentals was, of course, a valuable financial stabilizer.

The theatre proper, attached to the office building, ran 155 feet eastward along Twenty-third Street. Its granite façade (which was actually the *side* of the theatre), elaborately decorated in the then fashionable French Renaissance style, was a cause of wonder and controversy. Launt Thompson, the sculptor, thought it "magnificent . . . as solid as ornamental," and wrote later from Europe that he preferred it to the Paris Opéra.[56] A less cordial observer, finding it a hodgepodge of second-hand ideas, declared it "as dead as Julius Caesar."[57] Seventy feet tall to the cornice line, it was topped by an approximately 35-foot mansard section and three broad towers rising somewhat higher. The westernmost section of the façade contained the main public entrance, nobly arched; the eastern section contained the stage door.

From Twenty-third Street one stepped into the main lobby and turned left into the auditorium (or mounted stairs to the balconies).[58] The auditorium, although in fact

55 Launt Thompson, the sculptor, attempted to engage the interest of the artists; see Thompson's many letters to Booth at The Players and transcriptions of Booth's letters to Thompson at the Theatre Collection of the New York Public Library.

56 Launt Thompson to Booth, 9 November 1868, and 7 January 1869, The Players.

57 The *World* (New York), 4 February 1869.

58 Many accounts of the interior of the theatre, giving conflicting

a rectangular room about 75 feet across and 70 feet deep, gave the impression from its curved balconies of a horseshoe shape. The main floor seated 576 persons, the first balcony 441, the second balcony 331, the third balcony 443: a total of 1771. Six proscenium boxes accommodated another 40 or 50, and there was standing room for about three hundred. At prices ranging from 50 cents to $1.50, the house could hold upwards of $2400—though, to be sure, it was seldom filled to capacity and a nightly receipt in excess of $2000 was rare.

The decoration, executed by Italian artists in marble, scagliola, and fresco, featured ceiling paintings of scenes from classical mythology and from Shakespeare. Busts and reliefs of famous past actors and playwrights abounded. A gorgeous chandelier hung from the center of the ceiling. Sight-lines and acoustics were accounted remarkable in every part of the house. Ventilation and heating were controlled by a huge fan mounted in the space above the ceiling; it pulled warmed or cooled air into the house through apertures under the seats, and expelled the used air over the rooftop. Fire-protection was well-nigh absolute.

The stage house was revolutionary in design and purpose. Booth replaced the traditional split-scene, or wing-and-groove, method of scene-changing with the rise-and-sink method. His stage house rose 90 feet or more above the stage floor so that scenes could be flown down (in the modern manner); and under the stage was a 32-foot-deep cellarage, from which scenes could be thrust up through slits in the stage floor. The rise and fall of scenes was smooth and soundless, the machinery being powered by the flow of

---

dimensions, appeared in the metropolitan newspapers at the time Booth's Theatre opened. For the best-balanced account see Winter, *Life and Art*, pp. 82-90. The figures on seating capacity are taken from Honaker, *Edwin Booth*, p. 104.

water from great tanks on the roof. The stage space was immense—76 feet from wall to wall and 55 feet deep. The proscenium opening, some 50 feet wide and much taller than wide, allowed only 12 or 13 feet of wing space at either side, but since most of the scenery moved vertically more wing space was not needed. To the south of the stage (off stage left) was a vast paint-room, 55 feet long, 30 feet tall, and 16 feet wide. Above the paint-room were two dozen or more dressing rooms, including a lounge or reception-room for the star.

In early January of 1869, when Booth was half-mad with worry over last-minute preparations for the opening, the Robertson brothers acted out a cunning offstage drama of their own devising.[59] Richard absented himself from the premises for several days. John looked blue. Then John began to complain to Booth, "in sighs and tears," about poor Richard's mental suffering. Now that the building was done, no one thought to reward Richard for all the labor and imagination he had poured into it, not even to praise him. The injustice of it all was figured in the very decoration of the building: wherever one looked, his eye fell on the letter "B" (Booth's initial); by rights the letter "R" should appear there also.

John's part was prologue. He withdrew and Richard took up the theme. On 13 January Richard sent Booth a long letter, whining and petulant, in which he claimed the moral right to ownership of half, or at the least three-sevenths, of the physical property: "If it had not been for your desire to have all this in your name—it would have started right in the first place—we should have bought the land together and divided the profits accruing from your advantages in a proper proportion. This is the way the enterprise should

[59] The following narrative is derived from Booth to J. H. McVicker, 18 February 1876.

have commenced and it is the way it should be treated now."[60] They had an interview. Richard was living in daily terror, he said. For Booth's sake he had drawn larger amounts on the credit of Treadwell and Company than had been authorized. At any moment the company might close on him. Friends would not help him because he could show no real security, nothing but promises and paper. And one night lately as he was brooding by the fireside, his ten-year-old boy Aussie had asked him, "Papa, what do you *own* of Booth's Theatre?" The question had struck him dumb, for he had been asking himself that very thing. He could only answer the child, "Nothing."

He presented a memorandum of the money he had invested and the notes he had signed. The whole amounted to $400,000, or about one-third of the $1,200,000 which the theatre is supposed finally to have cost.[61] Could not Booth do him justice and save his credit by granting him title to a fair share of the property? Bewildered by the arithmetic, blinded by sympathy, utterly taken in by his "maudlin twaddle," Booth capitulated. "He struck at the proper moment," Booth said later, "just as my fire was hottest with contending influences blowing me to a white heat. To get that theatre open I would have said *Yes*, had he asked me for *all* of it." Shortly thereafter, though Magonigle advised him not to, he deeded away three-sevenths of his property —made Robertson a "free gift" of it "in consideration of his

---

[60] Robertson's letter is printed in Lockridge, *Darling of Misfortune*, pp. 191-193.

[61] No one knows what the cost really was. As Harry Magonigle explained to J. H. McVicker—9 February 1876, The Folger Shakespeare Library—Joseph Booth, who was keeping the books during the period of building, mixed into the building accounts all the production costs of two plays, and these cannot be separated. Magonigle conservatively estimated the costs of land and building at $975,500. When Booth gives the figure of $1,200,000 he is probably reckoning in interests and other hidden costs.

superhuman efforts in getting me into his clutches thus securely."[62]

Next came brother John's turn. Richard pointed out that John had saved them thousands by his astute economies in supervising the construction. Surely he deserved recompense. A gift of, say, $30,000 would be appropriate. Booth says that he was "knocked flat-a-back" at this proposal, for he believed that John had been on the architect's payroll all the while; but apparently he capitulated on this point also.

This was not the end of the wretched Robertson story. In the spring of 1871, Robertson attempted to buy Booth out. Booth's policy of "high art," he argued, was dooming them to failure. If he could manage the place alone he would turn it into a popular variety house, like Niblo's, and succeed. Booth's investment, he acknowledged, amounted at that moment to $400,000. He offered Booth, not cash, but $250,000 worth of property which he did not own. Booth declined. In the fall of 1871 Robertson asked Booth to buy *him* out. At that time, according to the account book, his share was worth $264,374.80, but he was willing to sacrifice it for a mere $240,000. So Booth, who had made him a "free gift" of the property into which Robertson had in fact put nothing, now must pay him nearly a quarter of a million to get rid of him. Having no ready cash he signed over masses of valuable real estate in New Jersey, Harlem, and Connecti-

---

[62] The "Booth's Theatre Account Books" would seem to disprove Booth's story: it was recorded on 1 February 1869 that Booth *sold* Robertson three-sevenths of the property for the sum of $170,000. But this, I believe, is merely a fiction of bookkeeping. It does not mean that any money changed hands, but only that Robertson's supposed investment of $400,000 (which, by the way, Harry Magonigle puts at $350,000) was reduced by the supposed payment of $170,000. Incidentally, the account books reveal that at several of the quarterly balancings in 1869-71, while the partnerships lasted, Robertson *overdrew* his share of the profit account in amounts ranging from $1200 to nearly $20,000.

cut, and signed a bill of indebtedness of $39,500, to be paid in four years. And Robertson, still owning his tack factory, joined the flock of creditors who drove Booth into bankruptcy three years later.

THE FIRST CAMPAIGN at Booth's Theatre began in midseason, on 3 February 1869. *Romeo and Juliet* played nine and a half weeks and *Othello* seven weeks, both plays featuring Booth and Mary McVicker. At the end of May, Booth's leading man, Ned Adams, took over, starring at first in stock pieces, then in a dramatization of *Enoch Arden*, which ran through the summer to the end of July.[63]

Booth chose *Romeo and Juliet* as his opener for a constellation of reasons. It had been ready to go on in a new production when the Winter Garden burned, and Booth wished to emphasize the continuity of his producing program. With its fourteen scenes of life in medieval Verona it would exploit fully the spectacular potential of his new stage and its rise-and-sink method of scene change. He wanted to show off Mary McVicker ("the best actress we've had for a century in this country") in what he took to be her strongest role. He had prepared his own "true version" of the text, which (though neither as novel or as true as he thought it to be) would win him some measure of prestige as a "restorer."

In its 58 performances *Romeo & Juliet* brought in nearly $84,000[64]—a profit, William Winter says, of over $60,000.[65]

---

[63] For the Booth's Theatre repertory, 1869-73, see G.C.D. Odell, *Annals of the New York Stage*, VIII, pp. 422-428, 565-570; IX, pp. 8-11, 141-146, 254-259.

[64] Actually $83,887.70. This is the total of the performance-by-performance receipts as recorded in the "Nightly Receipts: Booth's Theatre, 1869-73" at The Players. All figures of receipts which I give or estimate hereafter are drawn from these volumes.

[65] Winter, *Life and Art*, p. 98.

I doubt Winter's cheerful statistic. If we count running expenses at $800 a night—the lowest figure Booth gives for the expense of a large-cast tragedy[66]—the profit figure is cut back to some $37,500. And this allows nothing for the cost of the mounting, which had been over a year in preparation. The real profit must have been under $20,000.

Yet profit there was, and large houses, and Booth may well have been elated at this triumph of the "legitimate." He could not, though, have taken much pleasure in the critical response to his own performance or Miss McVicker's. The critics were not brutal toward the lady, but they were firm. As the *Herald* said, she "is not a delicate geranium rising from a Sevres vase. She is a strong, practical Western, little woman, with but little artistic training, but a great deal of raw vigor and rude force; and, while she can never realize the graceful, buoyant, lovely Juliet of Shakespeare's creation, we have no doubt she would manage Romeo's business after marriage with considerable effect."[67] Some of them *were* brutal toward Booth. "Mr. Booth can't play Romeo," declared one critic, "and knows it probably as well as we do."[68] Others ridiculed his goggling eyes, his writhing from head to foot "like a jointed snake," his clogging about the stage "as though emulous of the saltatorial fame of Lotta," his howling in the love scenes.[69] It was, indeed, Booth's very worst part, and after this run he never played it again.

The scenery carried the day. "Of the scenery," said the *World* critic,

---

[66] In a letter to Lawrence Barrett, 25 October 1870, now at The Players, Booth reckoned the nightly expenses of a lightly cast play like Jefferson's *Rip Van Winkle* at $600 to $700; of a tragedy at $800 to $850.

[67] The *Herald* (New York), 8 February 1869.

[68] *Spirit of the Times*, 6 February 1869.

[69] The *Herald* (New York), 8 February 1860.

nothing can be said in praise that is not justified. Scene painting in such hands as those of Messrs. Witham and Hilliard becomes a fine art. . . . In the first scene we have not a house, nor a row, but a whole square of the Gothic architecture of Italy reproduced with a pains and a patience which would have brought forth plaudits if only a tithe of it had been exhibited. . . . The balcony-scene is exquisite. The stage is an Italian garden surrounded by brick and marble walls, . . . and Juliet's balcony, just seen at the right, is an exquisite and faithful bit of architecture. The facade of a Romanesque church, at least forty feet high, backs the square upon which Mercutio meets his death. The only bad scene is Juliet's bower, which is a monstrous melange of utterly impossible roses. But this is but a blemish upon a whole gallery of superb pictures.[70]

It was obvious, the writer implied, that Booth meant to devote to Shakespeare the scenic splendors wasted at rival theatres on such prurience as *The White Fawn* and Offenbach's *Genevieve*—"that he has an artistic aim beyond the mere catching of coppers."

The second production was supposed to have been *The Winter's Tale*, modelled after Charles Kean's famous archaeological recovery of ancient Syracuse. But whether the scenes were not ready, or for reasons of economy, *The Winter's Tale* was displaced by *Othello*. It ran for forty-two nights. Again the mounting was acclaimed and the acting blamed, though not so severely as before. Miss McVicker's ungentle Desdemona was no more gratifying than her hard Juliet. Booth acted well but he lacked the stature for Othello, and Ned Adams was too guileless for Iago. When they exchanged roles the play seemed in better balance, for Adams was the taller and heavier of the two, and Iago had

[70] The *World* (New York), 4 February 1869.

long been one of Booth's very best parts. For three weeks the box office held at $1500 to $1600 a night, then dropped to $1300, then to $1000 or under. Overall, presumably, there was a decent profit.

With the end of Booth's engagement, the receipts dropped sharply. Ned Adams was a pleasant man and a charming actor, but who would give up June evenings to watch a second stringer? The nightly receipts for his *Lady of Lyons* were less than $460. *Enoch Arden*, in a pretty production of a brand-new play on a most popular subject,[71] started out bravely at $1000 a night but soon levelled off at $700 or under, and the profits for its six weeks' run were small. Never again would Booth keep the house open through the whole summer.

The program of the second season (1869-70) reverted to the old Winter Garden pattern, which Booth hoped to perpetuate: a series of visiting stars in the autumn, his own work at the height of the season, and a shorter series of visitors to round the season off. It began on 2 August with Joe Jefferson's *Rip Van Winkle*, which did great business for seven weeks. Witham created for it a splendid *mise en scène*, and Jefferson's performance was described as "the purest, the truest and the noblest illustration of human nature and human sentiment that the present stage affords. . . . It more nearly approaches positive perfection than any single piece of acting now before the public."[72] In spite of the "intolerably hot" weather,[73] the nightly receipts leaped well above $1600, and stayed there throughout its seven

[71] This version of *Enoch Arden* was by Julie de Margueritte. An improved version by Arthur Matthison (*French's Standard Drama*, no. CCCLXXVII) was produced at Booth's Theatre, with Theodore Hamilton, on 25 September 1869.

[72] The *Times* (New York), 3 August 1869.

[73] The "Nightly Receipts" frequently reports weather and street conditions.

weeks. Then came Kate Bateman, in the prime of her power, for ten weeks of moral melodrama—*Leah the Forsaken* and *Mary Warner*: a profitable engagement, averaging in most weeks from $1100 to $1300 a night. In December the venerable James Hackett made his last major stand as Falstaff; but the world was weary of Hackett, and after a good first week he barely made expenses.

The public was waiting for the return of Booth. On 5 January he opened his greatest production of *Hamlet*.[74] This was in essence a revival of the Winter Garden *Hamlet*, but now developed so monumentally in the vast spaces of the new stage that audiences and critics accepted it as wholly new. Its first three weeks drew over $2300 a night, the strongest sustained pull in the whole time of Booth's management. By the eighth and ninth weeks it dropped to about $1100, but it rose again to the $2300 level in its last performances. Booth withdrew it after 64 nights. On 28 March, after a week of stock plays, he offered his second full-fashioned revival of the season—*Macbeth*. Physically he was inadequate to Macbeth, however, nor was the *mise en scène* especially remarkable. Three weeks of it brought his own engagement to a close.

The rest of the season was largely a family affair, and it was a sorry letdown. John Clarke had returned from London, where he had gone to live, presumably to attend to affairs of the Walnut Street Theatre (including buying up Booth's share in it); and although nothing in Clarke's repertory of old-fashioned farce could honestly qualify in a theatre devoted to "high art" Booth gave him a six weeks' run. For one week (18-23 April) the public hailed him as an old favorite with houses of $1400 and better, but the attraction faded and receipts dropped to under half that figure.

[74] For a full account of this *Hamlet* production, see Shattuck, *The Hamlet of Edwin Booth.*

From comic brother, then, to comic father. James Mc-Vicker, who had not even the advantage of a New York following, played two weeks of *Taking the Chances* to an average of barely $250. Last of all an "old favorite," Ada Clifton, in three weeks of melodrama drew even worse houses. The account books from mid-May to early July record an overall loss to the management of $17,083.94.[75]

During his third season (1870-71) Booth economized by reducing the number of guest stars and consequently the number of new productions to be mounted. The previous year there had been seven guests, this year there were two. Joe Jefferson returned in mid-August to open the season with Rip Van Winkle (the scenery all built and paid for) and held the stage for the remarkable number of 149 performances, down to 7 January. For six weeks his usual receipts were above $1500, and although in November and December they dropped below $1000, the overall profits were apparently in excess of $30,000.

On 9 January Booth returned, not adventurously but wisely, with a splendid new production of *Richelieu*, which had long since been proved his second-strongest card. Witham's scenery was praised on all sides for its beauty, historical fidelity, and realistic detail. The drawing-power of *Richelieu* never approached that of *Hamlet*, but it brought in nearly $1700 a night for two weeks, $1100 for four weeks, and nearly $1500 for the last two weeks. On 6 March Booth offered a new production of *Much Ado*. This was a bad choice: his Benedick pleased not much better than his Romeo, and after two weeks he dropped it. A revival of *Othello* could not rouse the public. Three weeks of mixed repertory brought Booth's work to a close on 22 April.

[75] "Booth's Theatre Account Books," entry at 22 July 1870.

Now came a great gamble. For over a dozen years Booth had been urging his friend Lawrence Barrett, who had achieved starring status in the provinces, to seek a foothold in New York City; in January of this 1871 season he had taken him into his own company.[76] For Barrett there was danger in this, for stars ceased to shine when they played second parts. But Barrett was so eager to join Booth that he swallowed pride, dismissed caution, and accepted leading-man status. The arrangements looked propitious. His weakest assignments would be De Mauprat in *Richelieu* and Don Pedro in *Much Ado*. On Saturday nights he would star in *The Marble Heart* and other plays from his own repertory. In *Othello* he would alternate with Booth as hero and villain. His great chance would come during the final months of the season. Booth had long intended to bring out *The Winter's Tale*, had in fact had most of the scenes painted two years earlier, and now he would turn the production over to Barrett. Barrett, adept in the caustic style, had long wanted to play Leontes. Out of this happy conjunction surely nothing but good could come. And furthermore, Booth would produce Barrett's favorite new play, W. G. Wills' *The Man o' Airlie*.

The results were disastrous. Although at the beginning of Barrett's engagement the critics praised him warmly in his leading-man functions, the public simply would not accept him as a star. His Saturday nights were embarrassing. In a week when *Richelieu* was regularly drawing $1200, *The Marble Heart* was worth a mere $400. *The Winter's Tale*, for all its novelty and all the care that Hilliard

---

[76] The early friendship of Booth and Barrett and the tangled relationships leading up to their estrangement at the end of 1872 are to be traced through their correspondence preserved at The Players. Another mass of Booth's letters to Barrett, written during their partnership in the 1880's, is in the Harvard Theatre Collection.

and Witham had spent upon its mounting, never once drew $1000, and its average over the six weeks' run was exactly $547. *The Man o' Airlie,* which would someday be recognized as Barrett's finest vehicle, averaged in its thirty-one nights a shameful $286. It cost Booth $18,500 to serve his friend.[77]

Two seasons in succession, then, had collapsed in their final months—one with unworthy plays and players, one with supposedly strong attractions. It was at this point that co-manager Robertson began to interfere: could they not go after the crowds with shows of really popular appeal? Booth was angered at being told his business by one who "knew nothing," but "to humor him" he consented to open the fourth season (1871-72) with six weeks of the banjo-playing, clog-dancing, much-loved doll hoyden, Lotta Crabtree. As William Winter put it, Lotta's kind of art was "inappropriate to a classic theatre"[78]—a very mild distillation of Booth's opinion in the matter. He was evidently more relieved than distressed that her average draw was only $900.

Meanwhile he had arranged a bold counterstroke. The aging lioness Charlotte Cushman, lately returned from long sojourn in Europe, was available and he must have her. Although her heavily masculine style was no longer in the front line of fashion, her unimpeachably "classic" Shakespearean acting would restore the balance after the follies of Lotta. The Cushman, however, was a fierce bargainer.[79] Refusing flatly to play on shares, she bullied Booth into paying her $500 a night: counting an extra fee for the Saturday

[77] So Booth tells Barrett in a letter of 7 March 1872, now at The Players.

[78] Winter, *Life and Art,* p. 124.

[79] Miss Cushman's many letters arguing over the conditions of this engagement are preserved at The Players. Annotations by Booth indicate the substance of his replies.

matinee, she prised out of him $3250 a week. Her agreement called for three weeks of Queen Katharine and three weeks of Lady Macbeth. To cut costs Booth signed on the inexpensive but tiresome William Creswick to support her. The lioness howled at this indignity: "Oh *dont* dont give me Creswick for Macbeth. I shall have to carry the play & something else if you do." But he did. In the long run she made her point by cutting back Lady Macbeth to a single week and by completing her engagement, without benefit of Creswick, with two weeks of Meg Merrilies. Her receipts averaged nearly $1200 a night, well above Lotta's, yet they brought little gain to the treasury.[80]

What gain there was was forthwith lost on the November visitor, John E. Owens, a competent but undistinguished comedian in the homely-sentimental line, a minor species of the genus Joe Jefferson. At the end of November Booth noted gloomily that his season's profit to that date was exactly $49.[81]

For three weeks of December he marked time with his own *Hamlet,* and then on Christmas night he opened what would be the last really memorable Shakespearean revival of his management—*Julius Caesar,* with himself as Brutus, Barrett as Cassius, and the flamboyant Frank Bangs as Antony. Scenically splendid, vastly acclaimed, it reverberated down the century. In 1876 Jarrett and Palmer, who acquired the scenery when they took over Booth's theatre, revived it for a distinguished run, starring Barrett and Davenport. In the latter 1880's it figured largely (though with diminished *mise en scène*) in the Booth-Barrett tour-

[80] A year later when she sought a return engagement, Harry Magonigle told her that during her second, third, and fourth weeks the management had lost $2143.27, and that henceforth she must accept sharing terms—"Transcript Book of Magonigle's Business Correspondence," 5 November 1872, The Players.

[81] Booth to Lawrence Barrett, 29 November 1871, The Players.

ing repertory; and successive lesser starring actors owed much to Booth's precedent with the play. *Caesar* played for 85 performances, during which Booth took a turn at each of the three leading roles. For over five weeks it averaged better than $1200 a night, but in the final weeks it sank to the $600-to-$800 level.

From 25 March, Carlotta Leclercq lost money every night for a month in *As You Like It* and assorted modern comedies. On 1 May Booth offered a new production of *Richard III*—not Shakespeare restored, however, but the traditional Cibber version. This, since it starred Booth alone in a role he could sparkle in, drew business of $1200 and better for three weeks, down to 18 May, which was Booth's last night. Then Ned Adams returned to preside over the demise of the season (houses declining from $750 to $350) with a six-weeks' revival of *Enoch Arden.*

Booth was beaten, though he would persist through one more season, his fifth. His own contributions in 1872-73 were limited to a three weeks' repetition of *Richard III* in January, followed by two weeks of John Howard Payne's *Brutus.* His most memorable visitor was Adelaide Neilson, that "dream of love and beauty" as Odell calls her,[82] who in November made her American debut at Booth's as Juliet and Rosalind, and returned in May as Amy Robsart. His weakest draws were J. W. Wallack, aging and ailing, who opened the fall season with five weeks of humdrum work in *The Bells;*[83] and W. J. Florence playing *The Ticket of Leave Man* and *No Thoroughfare* in February and March.

[82] G.C.D. Odell, *Annals of the New York Stage*, IX, p. 256.

[83] Booth had engaged Wallack with the intention of starring him in Watts Phillips' *Marlborough*, not knowing that Wallack's actorship was ruined by ill-health. *Marlborough* was withheld, and Wallack died the following May. See Booth to Lawrence Barrett, 26 December 1872, and Magonigle to Watts Phillips, 11 September 1872, "Transcript Book," at The Players.

A total of one hundred twelve nights were given over to Dion Boucicault in his popular Irish melodramas—*Arrah-na-Pogue, Jessie Brown, Daddy O'Dowd,* and others. These drew very well at first, poorly at last, and on the whole mark a sorry decline from Booth's principles of "high art." Although the season's receipts did not fall notably below par, Booth must have recognized that such creeping gain would never wipe out his indebtedness. He was still nearly half a million dollars short of ownership of the theatre; he could find that sort of money only by full-time acting on the road. On 14 June 1873 he abandoned management altogether, leasing the theatre to his brother Junius.

With the financial crash in the fall of 1873, his creditors closed in. In January 1874 he declared bankruptcy. The vultures were at him, beak and claw, but this disaster and his rescue from debt by his father-in-law James McVicker are only aftermath, and need not concern us here.[84]

Booth would never touch management again.

IT WOULD BE idle to pretend, as apologists used to, that Booth's Theatre was not a failure. If the final responsibility of these "Players of a Perilous Game" is to "honor the arts of the stage," their *first* responsibility is to keep the enterprise going—to maintain the financial solvency which makes the honoring possible. That meant, in Booth's day, when the robber barons were just learning to rob and had not yet established great foundations to give their wealth away—that meant maintaining financial solvency in the market place.

This Booth could not do. He could not manage finances and affairs. His *earning* power was enormous, and throughout his career money flowed to him and from him in a

[84] McVicker's letters to Booth covering this aftermath are preserved at The Players.

golden stream. But he was wasteful. He threw away on real estate, mortgages, needless building costs, excessive production expense (not to mention his generous charities), money enough to have paid comfortably for his theatre long before he lost it. Impulsive and plunging, he would spend thousands on the project of the moment without care for the consequences, trusting that all would come right in the end. Accounts were kept, but he did not mind them. In his correspondence we find him overestimating profits with wild exaggeration, or not recognizing losses until months after they had occurred.[85] He could not take advice or delegate authority, but decided everything himself. And, as we have seen, he played into the hands of sharpers, almost asking to be plucked.

As we have also seen, he was damaged by the star system. The public demanded stars and the stars demanded money, sometimes more than they were worth. His attempts to promote lesser actors to starring status regularly failed, and he may even have harmed some of these intended beneficiaries of his goodwill by scheduling them for the lag-end of the season when the sated public would not give them a hearing. The timing of his own appearances was not strategic. Had he applied his personal drawing-power to the early or late months he might have bolstered the receipts of those weaker times; but he invariably offered his own most attractive production in midseason, at Christmas or soon thereafter, when audiences would have come to the theatre anyway.

[85] Thus he once claimed that his *Hamlet* averaged $2400 a night for its first five weeks—Booth to Lawrence Barrett, 15 October 1870, The Players. In fact it averaged $2522 the first week, and ran down to $1685 by the fifth, averaging $2104 throughout that time. Again, Barrett's plays in 1871 lost Booth $18,500, but he appears not to have recognized this fact until nearly a year later—Booth to Lawrence Barrett, 7 March 1872, The Players.

The loftiness of Booth's motives is not in question. He wanted to preserve the so-called legitimate drama in the American theatre, and to revivify it with *Art*. By "Art" he meant, for the most part, *mise en scène*, especially of the "historically accurate" kind. And, of course, his theatre was morally "pure": as William Winter put it, "intellectual and refined persons could find pleasure and benefit in the contemplation of it." But the success of his greater productions —*Hamlet, Richelieu, Julius Caesar*—depended very little upon these conservative principles. The moral argument (mere upside-down puritanism) often dribbled off the pens of journalists in those days, and might occasionally excuse theatre-going for the socially timid, but it was no cogent box-office lure. Nor was the investment in historicity worth as much as Booth expected it to be: historicity was not even original, for Booth was only transplanting to America what Macready and Kean had previously done in England; his American audiences, less schooled in historical tradition than the English, were correspondingly less impressed by it. They gave it quick looks and lip service, but what they really craved was great acting, especially Booth's acting. When in the summer of 1870 young Charles Clarke put together his two hundred-page description of Booth's Hamlet,[86] he spent hardly a dozen sentences on the scenery, which Booth and Witham had spent years in perfecting. Scenery for Clarke was nothing more than background to the experiencing of Booth's performance, to what "Booth has done to drill my mind, and put an edge upon my sensibility; and instruct my emotions, and inform my imagination."

Booth's genius lay in acting. His brooding Brutus, the crimson flash of his Richelieu, the wit of his Iago, his manic

[86] The Folger Shakespeare Library.

passion in Bertuccio, the sweet deep mystery of his Hamlet —these enthralled our grandfathers: their images haunt us still. Booth's release from management—his failure, if we call it that—set him free to spread these images into every part of the land.

Wyndham of Wyndham's

GEORGE ROWELL

THE PRACTICE of naming theatres after theatre people is uncommon in England. Perhaps this state of affairs reflects the nation's adherence to monarchy. Playhouses have been called after kings, queens, princes, princesses, and even mere dukes and duchesses since the Restoration, but although the circus, that most democratic temple of the the arts, began to honor its Astleys, Davises, and Henglers from the end of the eighteenth century, the first English actor to give his name to a theatre was the comedian J. L. Toole, who rechristened the Charing Cross Theatre in 1882. His lead was followed by Edward Terry (no relation to Ellen) when building his own theatre in 1888, and in fairly rapid succession there appeared the Garrick, a post-humous issue, Daly's, and the Hicks, now the Globe. But alone among the London theatres Wyndham's still bears the name of the actor-manager who built it, Charles Wyndham, born Charles Culverwell, and later Dr. Culverwell, Member of the Royal College of Surgeons, Doctor of Medicine of the German University of Giessen.

Wyndham (who adopted this as his stage name while still an amateur and legalized it in 1886), although born in 1837, the year of Victoria's accession, had more in common with the Edwardian actor-manager than with the Victorian "stroller." As his medical degrees suggest, he came from a professional background, although he seems to have practiced medicine only briefly, as a surgeon in the United States Army during the Civil War. The family had German connections; Wyndham's first wife was of German origin, and he himself spoke German well enough to play David

Garrick successfully in German, both in Berlin and in Moscow and St. Petersburg.

Wyndham's career diverged from those of his fellow Victorian actors in other ways. Coming from a nontheatrical family, he took to professional acting comparatively late; one consequence was that he lacked the versatility which characterized the Victorian theatrical dynasties: the Keans, Terrys, Websters, Wigans. In this respect he served the same tough apprenticeship as did Henry Irving, a year his junior, and their early careers were interestingly entwined: they sometimes shared a dressing room, and on one occasion a leading lady ten years their junior but ten times as experienced, Ellen Terry.[1] One dark December morning in Liverpool they even shared a theatrical agent's waiting room, and discovered that they were rivals for the same job. In the discussion that followed a window was broken, Wyndham collected the bill, and Irving collected the job.[2]

But as actors in the making the two were quite different, and it was Wyndham who marked the exception, Irving the rule. The standard fare of the Victorian playbill was Shakespeare and spectacular melodrama, and in these Irving, for all his peculiarities of diction and gait, came to excel. Wyndham, on the other hand, never played Shakespeare in London (and only in his salad days elsewhere), while his early efforts at melodrama were received unequivocally enough to warn him to desist. One paper kindly attributed his Irish accent as Shaun-the-Post in *Arrah-na-Pogue* to "a slight cold,"[3] while another declared roundly it was "enough to cause a Fenian rising."[4] At that stage of his

1 At the Queen's Theatre, London, October 1867-January 1868.

2 Percy Hutchinson (Wyndham's nephew), *Masquerade* (London, 1936), p. 29.

3 *Era*, 5 November 1865. The performance was at the Amphitheatre, Liverpool, commencing 25 October 1865.

4 Wyndham's speech to the Twentieth Century Club, Chicago, 1890

career he lacked the technique a Victorian actor-of-all-work required, and though he proceeded to make sure of adequate training, it was training for his own "line of business," that of a "bustling" or "rattling" comedian in the dashing, impudent parts ("never pause for breath or the audience will stop laughing") that Charles James Mathews had made famous a generation earlier. In fact several of Mathews' "comediettas" found a regular place in Wyndham's repertoire, including such forgotten titles as *His Last Legs* and *Trying It On*, and later he tackled Mathews' part of Dazzle in *London Assurance*. Comedy and farce provided the "makeweight" of the Victorian playbill, and rarely stretched beyond a couple of acts. Their authors had no loftier aim than to please that section of the audience which came early or stayed late. Wyndham was largely instrumental in promoting farce to a full-length form, but the vehicles in which he achieved this were mostly of foreign manufacture, and consequently he added little of permanence to the English farcical repertory. While the historian may regret that he never appeared in a Pinero farce and only in a minor Gilbert, *Foggerty's Fairy*, there is ample evidence that he raised the second-hand farces he did play to first-class standards of performance. During the 1870's, when he ran the Criterion, he was known as "the electric light comedian." It is an illuminating description.

If Wyndham had been limited as an actor to farce, his name might now be interred with those who specialize in this most ephemeral form of drama: a Lamb may immortalize Munden, a Lewes may conjure up Charles

---

(a source of varying reliability), reported in the *Chicago Tribune*, 18 January 1890, p. 1. See also Mary Moore, *Charles Wyndham and Mary Moore*, "printed for private circulation" (1925), pp. 39-42. The second Lady Wyndham's book is a very rare item, but an invaluable account of Wyndham's later career.

James Mathews, but who today has heard of, still less read, *The Turnpike Gate* or *Cool as a Cucumber*? Fortunately for Wyndham, his style matured as he matured. Although his voice could never do justice to poetry, and some always found it harsh, he came to command a rich vein of pathos. Henry Arthur Jones, who was to supply most of his final successes, wrote with gratitude as well as authority: "He'd only two notes in his voice, but he could do anything with them,"[5] while W. L. Courtney, writing in the *Daily Telegraph* after the actor's death, elucidated the paradox a little further: "Nine men out of ten would tell you that Wyndham's voice was harsh and unmusical; nineteen women out of twenty would tell you that it was the most compelling and seductive thing in the world."[6] Thus, when middle age finally overtook him, he was able to drop the frenzied pace of farce and turn to the more leisurely gait of romantic comedy, in particular to Robertson's David Garrick, the part with which he is most closely associated. When the supply of romantic revivals ran out, he was still able to keep up with public taste, as the worldly-wise but infinitely compassionate *raisonneur* of the Society comedies Jones and others wrote for him. It was as Sir Richard Kato, Sir Christopher Deering, and Sir Daniel Carteret that he inspired the government to create him Sir Charles Wyndham, and on the proceeds of these Society comedies he was able to make himself Wyndham of Wyndham's.

If the building of this theatre insures his place in English theatre history, his niche in the American theatre, though more modest, is no less singular. This is not the occasion to tell in detail the story of his army service, although for some fourteen years the *Oxford Companion to the Theatre* be-

[5] Doris Arthur Jones, *Life and Letters of Henry Arthur Jones* (London, 1930), pp. 209-210.

[6] See also his *The Passing Hour* (London, 1925), pp. 202-203.

lieved him to have enlisted on the Confederate side. As a surgeon he spent his time mostly in base hospitals, in or near St. Louis, Philadelphia, and New York.[7] He did see active service throughout the Red River campaign in Louisiana and Texas, and relates that he lost his brand-new uniform "for entering captured cities" during the retreat from Springfield Landing in April 1864.[8] Even this chapter of his career is not without theatrical interest, for he twice interrupted his military service to assault the American stage, on the first occasion at Grover's Theatre, Washington, as Osric to the Hamlet of John Wilkes Booth.[9] In American theatre history, however, his significance is chiefly that of an early touring manager, particularly his three years as leader of the Wyndham Comedy Company in the midwest.

This company came into existence in 1870, after Wyndham had played a season in New York with Lester Wallack. A modest summer tour of a few "dates" on the eastern seaboard with a forgotten comedy, *The Lancers*, encouraged him to increase his repertory and his itinerary. With a nucleus of English actors he launched forth on a dauntingly extensive circuit bounded by Minneapolis and New Orleans. Joseph Jefferson, in his *Autobiography*, is specific about Wyndham's claim, with his, to precedence:

> After finishing an engagement in Chicago I decided to play in Detroit and other cities throughout Michigan where opera houses had lately been built; but as there were no stock companies attached to these new places,

[7] Acting Assistant Surgeon Culverwell's file is preserved amongst the records of the Surgeon General's Office in the National Archives, Washington, D.C. It refutes many legends regarding Wyndham's war service, e.g., that he was present at Gettysburg, Fredericksburg, and Chancellorsville (as even the *Times* obituary stated, 13 January 1919).

[8] Interview with Wyndham in the *World* (New York), 1 December 1889.

[9] 14 April 1863, announcement in the *Star* (Washington).

I engaged one for a short season to travel with me. In
Detroit I met Mr. Windham [*sic*] who was acting a play
called "The Lancers" there with a company of his own.
These were the first two combinations that I remember;
there may have been others before, but not to my
knowledge.[10]

Both Jefferson and Wyndham were dependent on the newly
evolved and evolving network of railroads, and to one modern Englishman at least the stamina of these pioneers rivals
that of their predecessors, the "strollers," especially as their
journeys were often made in extremes of weather. In February 1872, for example, Wyndham's company played at
Charleston and then, because of conflicting engagements,
had to divide, one section travelling on to Savannah and the
other, including Wyndham, heading at once for Detroit,
which they finally reached twelve hours late and an hour
after the curtain should have risen. The disappointed audience was just leaving the theatre as the weary comedians,
no doubt hungry and travel-stained, arrived. "Go back! Go
back! We're here! We've arrived!" they called to the dis-
persing crowd, and somehow contrived to put on a performance there and then.[11] On another occasion, while the
company was travelling from one engagement in St. Louis
to another in New Orleans the train was blocked by floods
at Grenada, Mississippi, whereupon they offered to give a
performance in the town hall. That auditorium, however,
proved to have no seats, so the citizens were urged to bring
their own, and heard the play from a rich variety of accom-

[10] *"Rip van Winkle": the Autobiography of Joseph Jefferson*, with a
Foreword by Eleanor Farjeon (London, 1949), pp. 249-250.

[11] T. Edgar Pemberton, *Charles Wyndham. A Biography* (London,
1904), p. 233. Pemberton wrote his book with some assistance from
Wyndham. It is, however, frequently inaccurate.

modation ranging between handsome *fauteuils* and humble kitchen stools, until at last each man crept home, snail-like, with his chair on his back.[12]

As its name suggests, the company played comedy although, less predictably, it was contemporary comedy of the Robertson "cup-and-saucer" variety. Wyndham's emergence as a leading London actor had coincided with the emergence at the Prince of Wales's Theatre under Squire Bancroft and his wife, Marie Wilton, of a brand of full-length comedy in which the technical resources of the Victorian theatre were lavished on the miniature canvas of the drawing room or parlor, rather than the spectacular scenes of Shakespeare and melodrama. For this advance Tom Robertson was responsible, both as author and "stage-manager," as his contemporaries called the director of the modern playbill. Robertson's plays *Ours* and *Caste* were the foundation of the Wyndham Comedy Company's repertory, which included such an up-to-the-minute piece in Robertson's style as *Two Roses*. This choice of delicate, atmospheric drama for what must of necessity have been a tough audience, educated mostly by experience, comes as a surprise, and certainly under the gruelling conditions of touring that Wyndham and his companions faced, there can have been little scope for the elaborate "stage-management" in which Robertson and the Bancrofts specialized. From time to time the midwestern public expressed its disappointment. Wyndham later quoted the views but never mentioned the identity of the town which received their performance with cries of, "What! Do you call *that* acting? You just sit about in chairs in the same kind of clothes as you go out in. Give us our money back!"[13] The fact remains

12 Pemberton, *Charles Wyndham*, p. 234.
13 Pemberton, *Charles Wyndham*, p. 72.

that the company were able to sit about in chairs and be paid for it over a period of three years.

Their base—inevitably—was Chicago, and they paid their first visit to Crosby's Opera House in March 1871. So popular did they prove that manager Crosby invited them to return in October, when he would be opening his splendid new theatre.[14] The date he had fixed for the opening was 9 October, and historians will need no reminder that the Great Chicago Fire broke out on 8 October. "If only I could have watched just one show in it" was poor Crosby's cry as he saw his dream burn down. It speaks volumes for the Chicago public that by November the Wyndham Comedy Company was playing at the Michigan Avenue Theatre, a converted drill hall, and that in January 1872 they were entrusted with the opening of the Chicago Academy of Music, the first theatre to be built after the Fire.

Nevertheless, there is evidence that a cup-and-saucer repertory, acceptable to the aspiring Chicago of 1871, proved cold comfort to the survivors of the Fire. The critic of the *Tribune*, blandly ignoring the success of an identical repertory exactly twelve months earlier expressed this view:

> The chief error made by Mr. Wyndham has been that of supposing with a small stock of plays, of a high order and bordering closely on the legitimate, that he could hold the favour of the public, and keep his coffers full. The attempt to do this in New York and Philadelphia has only been attended with moderate success. Chicago is a child among cities, and that style of management will not win

[14] Genevieve Goodman Johnson, "A History of the Chicago Theater, 1871-2" (M.A. thesis, University of Chicago) gives a useful account of the Wyndham Comedy Company in Chicago.

here as yet. The experience of the next decade will perhaps be different.[15]

Wyndham met this criticism by extending his repertory into the fields of melodrama and farce, most significantly with Bronson Howard's recent *Saratoga*, in which the manager reverted to his "bustling" style as Bob Sackett, the man with three fiancées, each in turn declared, sincerely if illogically, to be "My first and only love." Of all the plays Wyndham staged in these three years, *Saratoga* claimed his deepest loyalty. On returning to England he commissioned a fellow actor, Frank Marshall, to prepare an English version, which he produced as *Brighton*. On the success of this farce was built Wyndham's twenty-four-year reign at the Criterion Theatre, and on the benefits of that reign were built Wyndham's Theatre and the New Theatre, a unique family business in the English theatre world.

It may be acceptable at this point to look forward to Wyndham's subsequent American tours, and in particular to the precedent he established in 1883 by taking the Criterion Company, complete with scenery, costumes, and half a dozen plays, to San Francisco. This was the first visit paid by an English ensemble to the west coast, where earlier English actors, such as Charles Kean and Charles James Mathews, had merely "starred" with American companies. The visit followed a successful winter season at the Union Square Theatre, New York, and elsewhere on the east coast, playing a repertory of sophisticated farce, including *Brighton* and other Criterion favorites. The company's appearance in America preceded the first tour of Irving and Ellen Terry by a year, and may well have put the idea into Irving's head. It would be gratifying to report that San

[15] 16 June 1872.

Francisco gave Wyndham a pioneer's welcome, but the sad fact remains that the Criterion Company played to half-empty benches at the Bush Street Theatre and fared little better at the Baldwin, until in desperation Wyndham changed the bill to *Pink Dominos*, a risqué French adaptation, which San Francisco crowded to see.[16]

Wyndham paid further professional visits to North America in 1889, 1904, and 1909. One interesting feature of these later tours was the reluctance of the American public to accept him in the role of David Garrick, although by 1889 London had taken this performance permanently to its heart.[17] Both in New York and on tour Wyndham found American audiences loyal to him in farce but no less loyal to the memory of E. A. Sothern, their favorite, though adopted, son, who created Garrick in Robertson's play as well as Dundreary in Taylor's *Our American Cousin*. Wyndham's final tours were carried out under the management of the ubiquitous Charles Frohman, who must have shared with his star a gleeful satisfaction on reading the New York *Dramatic Mirror*'s comment after their opening night at the Lyceum in November 1904: "Sir Charles Wyndham's Garrick is well remembered by all the older American theatre-goers as perhaps the finest impersonation of this remarkably fine actor."[18] In 1909 and 1910 Wyndham, now over seventy, charmed New York and other American cities for the last time when he played the forty-five-year-old Tom Kemp in Hubert Henry Davies' miniature comedy, *The Mollusc*. Most appropriately, his final American performance was given at the National Theatre, Washington, on the site where almost fifty years earlier he

[16] *Morning Call* (San Francisco), 17 June 1883, p. 3.
[17] E.g., *Tribune* (Chicago), 8 January 1890: "He is not at his best in the role. . . . [He is] better in the rattling farces with which he has long been associated."
[18] 26 November 1904, p. 2.

had made his inauspicious American debut in support of John Wilkes Booth. The Old and New Worlds of the theatre can seldom have been so significantly linked.

However, returning to the Old World in the summer of 1872, Wyndham soon found that all trace of his modest success before joining Wallack had been effaced. His steady, if not spectacular, climb to artistic and financial eminence was very largely achieved by the popularity of his performance as Bob Sackett in *Brighton*. He first played the English version at the reconstructed Court Theatre in May 1874, and his success both in Sloane Square and on tour led, in December 1875 while he was playing *Brighton* at Brighton, to his receiving three telegrams. The first read,

Would you like to undertake management West End theatre?   Parravicini

The second read,

Would you go into management with me West End theatre?   Smale

The third read,

Can you open Criterion next Monday?
Alexander Henderson[19]

Henderson's offer qualified as the bird in the hand, worth two in the bushes of Smale or Parravicini. He had taken a lease of the diminutive Criterion Theatre earlier that year to promote his wife, Lydia Thompson, the burlesque star, but already found himself in need of an associate. On 27 December 1875 Wyndham opened at the Criterion in *Brighton*. He was to assume full control of the theatre in 1879 and to continue as its *raison d'être* until he built his own theatre in 1899. Even then he remained arbiter of the

[19] *Era*, 15 July 1899 (article on Wyndham to mark the end of his direct connection with the Criterion).

Criterion's policy, and in fact created his last success—Tom Kemp in *The Mollusc*—at the Criterion in 1907. When he died he had maintained control of the theatre for forty-four years, and his stepson, Sir Bronson Albery, assisted by his son, Donald Albery, still controls it. This record of family rule in a West End theatre wholly eclipses even that of the Kembles at Covent Garden.

The popularity of *Brighton* at the Court and the Criterion throws an interesting light on the taste of the London audience of the 1870's. Both playhouses reflect a new trend in theatre-building; both were small (the Criterion today holds 660) and had unexpected features. The Court was build in the outlying, though rapidly developing, district around Sloane Square, but was regarded as a West End theatre from the start. The Criterion stood at "the heart of the Empire," Piccadilly Circus, but was wholly underground, as it had been designed as a kind of basement to Spier and Ponds' restaurant. Even today the gallery is approached by descending a flight of steps, while the stalls are approached by descending several flights of steps. The playgoer who pauses to regain his breath may still notice the initials C. W. worked into the tiling of the staircase, a feature dating from the reconstruction of the theatre in 1884.

Clearly the building of such bandboxes as the Court and Criterion was inspired by the success of the Bancrofts in their Robertsonian repertory at the much older but equally small Prince of Wales's, and not surprisingly Wyndham, with three years' experience of the Wyndham Comedy Company, brought to the Criterion the standards of subtle, detailed presentation that the newly enlightened London audiences expected. On the other hand his programme was far removed from the gently romantic strain of *Ours* and *Caste*. The breakneck speed and attack of *Brighton* established Wyndham as a favorite of the London public, but it was the risqué *Pink Dominos* two years later that set the characteristic tone of Criterion farce—taken from the French but invariably defused in the process.

Perhaps this defusing can be illustrated by comparing a passage from *Pink Dominos* with its French original, *Les Dominos Roses*. In the exchange between Marguerite and Angélique, two wives who don the dominos of the title, Hénnequin and Delacour seem to be recalling Wycherley's Lady Fidget on the subject of Mr. Horner:

MARGUERITE: Aujourd'hui, l'espèce "mari" se devise en deux catégories: les adroits et les maladroits, ceux qui ne font pas pincer —et ceux—au contraire—qui—

ANGÉLIQUE: Ah! quelle horreur! (*Elle pose sa broderie*)

MARGUERITE: Il n'y en a pas d'autres—parmi les maris effectifs, bien entendu—parce que je ne te parle pas des invalides. Et encore, parmi ceux là, il y en a tant de faux—qui reprennent du service dans l'armée irrégulière.

The adaptor of *Pink Dominos*, by now something of a renegade from the Robertsonian mood of his *Two Roses*, was James Albery, who changed this passage to read quite harmlessly: "Show me the dog that won't take a bone. The only difference is the dog that is found out and the dog that isn't." Such changes do not merely indicate the stranglehold of the Lord Chamberlain on Victorian drama. They illustrate the curiously intermediate stage through which the English theatre was passing in the 1870's. The Bancrofts had attracted the educated classes back to the theatre but those classes did not choose to continue their education at

the play. This is true of all the farces Wyndham staged at
the Criterion, whether by old hands like Burnand and
H. J. Byron, or by new ones such as Albery, McCarthy or—
on one occasion—Gilbert. It is equally true of the totally
different fare offered by Irving at the Lyceum, Hare at the
Court, the Kendals at the St. James's, and D'Oyly Carte at
the Opera Comique and later the Savoy. The Criterion was
a civilized theatre: Wyndham was the first London manager to offer his audiences coffee in the intervals as well as
strong liquor, and to sell them specially designed pro-
grammes instead of playbills. But in the 1870's his enterprise did not—perhaps could not—go as far as stretching
their minds.

Where Wyndham was concerned this intermediate phase
extended into the 1880's, but took on a rather different appearance. With middle age approaching, the "electric light
comedian" could not hope to shine, or bustle or rattle, quite
so brightly. He was, however, fortunate in retaining and
even increasing his romantic appeal as the years passed.
Thus he began to look for classical comedies in which his
farcical image could be enhanced by an aura of period
romance. Among these classics were, predictably, *The
School for Scandal* (though not *The Rivals*) and *She Stoops
To Conquer*, as well as, less predictably, O'Keefe's *Wild
Oats* and Robertson's *David Garrick*. This last-mentioned
play, which Wyndham revived at the Criterion in 1886, provided him with an especially grateful part, at least as far as
British (as well as German and Russian) audiences went,
and in it he made his final appearance at the age of seventy-
six. The theatrical idol who is persuaded to feign drunken-
ness at a dinner to disabuse a young admirer of her
infatuation, but of course succumbs to and marries the
young lady instead, was an ideal blend of the old Wyndham
(when pretending to be drunk) with the new (when break-

ing his Ada's heart, only to claim her hand and dry the audience's tears at the end). It is by no standards, including Robertson's own, a good play, but it was the right play at the right time for Wyndham, and for his new leading lady, Mary Moore. Married at sixteen to James Albery, she had now found herself with three young sons and an increasingly undependable husband. Her rise in Wyndham's company from an obscure understudy to a star in her own right cannot be detailed here, but her acting ability as well as her acute business sense were among the foundation stones on which Wyndham's ultimate eminence rested.

By the 1890's the English stage was ready for a further step forward, which in Wyndham's case would make him independent of both adaptation and revival. In the commercial theatre this decade was marked by the evolution of "Society drama," a marriage of convenience between the fatal female of melodrama and the aristocrat with bachelor chambers in Albany, thus pleasing the affluent patrons of the stalls while retaining the loyalty of the pit and gallery. It was with this formula that Alexander established himself at the St. James's, and (to some extent) Tree at the Haymarket. Wyndham's particular achievement was to foster the talents of Henry Arthur Jones, hitherto an exponent of heavy drama, such as *The Silver King*, until he became a skilled exponent of high comedy.

Wyndham produced five of Jones's plays in all, and three of these, *The Case of Rebellious Susan*, *The Liars*, and *Mrs. Dane's Defence*, were major triumphs for both author and actor-manager. They contributed to the flowering of a species of Society comedy comparable in many respects to that of Etherege and Shadwell, forerunners of the Restoration school. By reproducing the accents and habits of the fashionable London set, Jones allowed Wyndham, by now a frequent guest of the Prince of Wales at Marlborough

House, to mirror on the Criterion's stage the elegant company who assembled in the stalls, and hold up the likeness for the admiration of the bourgeoisie in the dress circle.

These three plays also chart an interesting curve in the graph of the playwright's views, to be read against the constant of Victorian convention. It is clear that in the earliest of the three Jones intended Lady Susan Harabin to pay back her husband's infidelities by making full use of the opportunity offered her on a moonlight night in Cairo by the attentive Lucien Edensor. But this brand of sexual algebra would have been unacceptable even to the Wyndham of *Pink Dominos*, and was anathema to the guest of the Prince of Wales. Wyndham's correspondence with Jones reveals his determination to save Lady Susan's—and the Criterion's—good name. He is writing from St. Moritz two months before the production of the play:

> I stand as bewildered today as ever at finding an author, a clean-living, clear-minded man, hoping to extract laughter from an audience on the score of a woman's impurity. I can realise the picture of a bad woman and her natural and desirable end being portrayed, but that amusement pure and simple should be expected from the sacrifice of that one indispensable quality in respect for womanhood astounds me.
>
> I am equally astounded at a practical long-experienced dramatic author believing that he will induce married men to bring their wives to a theatre to learn the lesson that their wives can descend to such nastiness, as giving themselves up for one evening of adulterous pleasure and then returning safely to their husband's arms, provided they are clever enough, low enough, and dishonest enough to avoid being found out.[20]

[20] Letter in possession of Sir Bronson Albery, reprinted in part in Doris Arthur Jones, *Life and Letters of Jones*, pp. 163-167.

This difference of opinion continued throughout rehearsals, and shortly before the first night Wyndham proposed a compromise in the crucial recriminatory passage between Lucien and Lady Susan. "I want you to expunge the line 'I should kill myself if anyone knew' and 'never boasted,'" he wrote to Jones, "leaving the line: 'You have never spoken of me to any of your men friends?' These in no way interfere with your plans, but they afford me an opportunity of overcoming my strong repulsion to the whole idea which must be as evident to you as it is painful to me—and will allow me to go into the part with good will. Failing this, I am beginning to feel that my participation in the piece will not only be useless, but positively dangerous."[21] It was in fact in this ambiguous form that the play was produced and published.

After *Rebellious Susan* Wyndham's battle was won, and Jones embraced Victorian convention with the fervor of a convert. In *The Liars* Lady Jessica Nepean is treated by her husband in much the same manner as Susan is, but Lady Jessica's rebellion takes the form of agreeing to elope with the famous explorer, Edward Falkner. However, the prospect of adultery in darkest Africa is one she cannot ultimately face, and Wyndham as Sir Christopher Deering spent most of the last act convincing her that "I've nothing to say in the abstract against running away with another man's wife! There may be planets where it is not only the highest ideal morality, but where it has the further advantage of being a practical way of carrying on society. But it has this one fatal defect in our country today—it won't work!"

By 1900, the date of *Mrs. Dane's Defence*, Jones had

[21] Letter in the possession of Sir Bronson Albery, reprinted in part in Doris Arthur Jones, *Life and Letters of Jones*, pp. 162-163.

become a stalwart of the establishment. Here the technically innocent Mrs. Dane has dared to allow young Lionel Carteret to lose his heart to her by concealing her identity and with it the scandal in which she was quite unwittingly involved as a governess in Vienna. Married bliss for her and Lionel is statutorily permissible and even psychologically possible, but Jones made Wyndham, as Lionel's foster-parent, expose Mrs. Dane in cross-examination and despatch her to widowed exile in Devon. This is rough justice even in the eyes of Lady Eastney, an old friend of Sir Daniel Carteret:

LADY EASTNEY: Oh aren't you Pharisees and tyrants, all of you? And don't you make cowards and hypocrites of all of us? Don't you lead us into sin, and then condemn us for it? Aren't you first our partners, and then our judges?

SIR DANIEL: The rules of the game are severe. If you don't like them, leave the sport alone. They will never be altered.

In these and other Society dramas Wyndham emerged as the *doyen* of *raisonneurs*: worldy-wise, sympathetic, impartial, but inexorable. It must have needed acting of genius to deal with Sir Christopher's ten-minute homily to Falkner and Lady Jessica in the last act of *The Liars*, when the audience would normally be groping for their wraps. However, Wyndham's part in these plays was never limited to that of a mere spokesman for Society like, for instance, Cayley Drummle in *The Second Mrs. Tanqueray*. For Sir Richard Kato, Sir Christopher Deering, and Sir Daniel Carteret, there was always a companionable widow or a childhood sweetheart in the cast to make them the happiest of men—and their audience the happiest of audiences—as the curtain fell. An actor-manager has his privileges.

Reference to *The Second Mrs. Tanqueray* may draw attention to Wyndham's neglect of Pinero as a purveyor of Society drama at the Criterion, although he did employ several secondary exponents of the genre, such as R. C. Carton and Haddon Chambers. In fact Pinero's gloomy tone and labored manner would not have suited the quicksilver technique of even the middle-aged Wyndham. But the third, and infinitely cleverest, architect of Society drama should have had a hearing at the Criterion, and for his best play. In the autumn of 1894 Wyndham accepted for production a new comedy by Oscar Wilde called *The Importance of Being Earnest*. The success of *Rebellious Susan* caused a postponement, and the sequel is revealed in Wyndham's letter to Jones, dated 18 February 1895:

You are probably aware that "The Importance of Being Earnest" was mine for production later on. You may remember my asking you once when you were likely to have another piece ready for me, and I had this in view at the time. "Guy Domville" failed so utterly and Alexander was in a "hole." Oscar Wilde came to me and asked whether I would let Alexander have "The Importance of Being Earnest," which would benefit Alexander and also enable Wilde to realise earlier than he could with me. I did so, hoping that our piece would run through the season. By one of those odd coincidences, however, from the day I promised to cede the piece our business fell; of course I kept my word. Now, if with the approaching thaw, the business doesn't jump up, I am out of my calculations, and shall be in want of a piece.[22]

[22] Letter in the possession of Sir Bronson Albery, reprinted in part in *The Letters of Oscar Wilde*, Rupert Hart-Davis, ed. (London, 1962), pp. 418-419n.

Wyndham's loss was Alexander's gain, at least in the long view. It could be argued that even at fifty-six Wyndham would have made a more engaging John Worthing than the younger but more stolid Alexander. Certainly Wyndham, unlike Alexander, remained loyal to Wilde at the time of his trial, and later visited him in Dieppe. On 24 July 1897 Wilde reported to Robert Ross: "I saw Wyndham yesterday: he came for three hours, and now I feel I can do the play pretty well, as he leaves me *carte-blanche* to pull it about as I like."[23] "The play" was an adaptation of Scribe's *Verre d'Eau* which Wyndham had commissioned from the broken Wilde, perhaps as a concealed form of charity. Certainly the work was never done.

The triumphs which Wyndham together with his fellow actor-managers enjoyed in Society dramas during the 1890's provided the Ibsenites with plenty of ammunition for their assault on the obscurantism of the English stage. It should be noted, however, that the most articulate of the Ibsenites yielded to none in his admiration for Wyndham's acting, however severely the *Saturday Review* took him to task for his choice of play. Indeed, Shaw claimed to have intended the part of Leonard Charteris in *The Philanderer* for Wyndham—the creator of Bob Sackett and star of *Pink Dominos*, one assumes, rather than the *raisonneur* of the Criterion—and admitted in the preface to *Plays Unpleasant*: "I had written a part which nobody but Charles Wyndham could act, in a play which was impossible at his theatre"; while Mary Moore writes of a presentation copy of Shaw's plays inscribed, "The Author's cry over his Comedies: '*Ah, si Charles Wyndham voulait, ou si les autres pouvaient.*' "[24] The wish is father to much thought.

---

23 *Letters of Wilde*, p. 626.
24 Moore, *Charles Wyndham*, p. 123.

Wyndham as Valentine? Wyndham as Dubedat? Perhaps. But never Wyndham as Henry Higgins.

The century reached its climax for Wyndham with an invitation to open a theatre named after him. The theatrical center of London was moving from the Strand to the newly opened Shaftesbury Avenue. A plot of land halfway between the two in the Charing Cross Road was available for development, but the ground landlord, the Marquis of Salisbury (who was also Prime Minister) would agree to the building of a theatre on the site only if Wyndham were entrusted with its management. Originally the project was to have been financed by business interests, but in the end Wyndham and Mary Moore between them found the capital, and Wyndham left the Criterion after almost a quarter of a century to open his own theatre on 16 November 1899 with the perennial *David Garrick*. His biggest success there was undoubtedly *Mrs. Dane's Defence*, but his most interesting production was probably the English premiere of *Cyrano de Bergerac*. Both Irving and Tree had negotiated for the rights of Rostand's play before Wyndham secured them and created the part in Stuart Ogilvie's translation, revised by Louis N. Parker, in April 1900.

It was perhaps asking too much of both Wyndham and his public that when over sixty he should succeed as the disfigured warrior-poet. He had never mastered the art of poetic drama, and he was not helped by the English version: "The lyrics are very bad—but they could easily be added" was Irving's comment when he made over Ogilvie's adaptation to Wyndham.[25] The additions which Parker supplied did not save the day. It could be argued that *Cyrano* is an untranslatable play—at least into English—but Parker

[25] Letter in the possession of Sir Bronson Albery.

was a poetaster, rather in the Stephen Phillips vein, on whom Wyndham tended to rely. He had already staged two of Parker's romantic pieces at the Criterion, *The Jest*, an unlikely essay in Renaissance resuscitation, and *Rosemary*, a Barrie-esque trifle which won general acceptance. But Wyndham in *Cyrano* was not acceptable, although Mary Moore, playing Roxane, records loyally: "On every performance in that last beautiful scene I was moved to tears, and I think there were many others in the cast who were similarly affected."[26]

Unluckily, the cast were not paying but being paid. What the public could and did accept was Wyndham as Sir Charles. The newly acquired social eminence of the theatrical profession found fitting acknowledgment in the knighthood conferred on Irving in 1895. There were insistent rumors circulating at the time of the Diamond Jubilee in 1897 that Bancroft and Wyndham were to be similarly honored, but when the list was issued Bancroft's name stood alone.[27] In Edward VII's Coronation year, 1902, Wyndham received unofficial notification that he would become the third actor-knight. The Coronation itself was postponed because of the King's serious illness, but the honors list was to be issued in June as planned. There was, therefore, a double measure of anxiety among Wyndham's circle when on the eve of the press announcement no confirmation had been received either at his home or at the theatre, but anxiety turned to congratulation when the Prime Minister's letter was discovered awaiting collection at the Garrick Club.[28]

In the following year another playhouse opened under

[26] Moore, *Charles Wyndham*, p. 139.
[27] Moore, *Charles Wyndham*, pp. 154-155.
[28] Moore, *Charles Wyndham*, p. 154.

Wyndham's direction. This was the New Theatre, built on an adjacent site to Wyndham's with a frontage in St. Martin's Lane, and the planners seem to have entertained an extraordinary notion that if the two theatres were set back to back a single labor force of stagehands would suffice: a forlorn hope even in pre-union days and totally impracticable since. The New Theatre was the last and largest of Wyndham's domains. It holds over a thousand and can stage spectacular productions on a scale impossible at the Criterion or Wyndham's. This feature justified itself triumphantly during the Second World War, when the New Theatre became the joint home of the Sadler's Wells Opera and the Old Vic for the historic seasons which established Laurence Olivier as the leader of the English stage. Wyndham and Mary Moore opened the theatre with a revival of *Rosemary* on 12 March 1903. Their own performances there were not numerous, but included one significant success: the delicate comedy *Captain Drew on Leave* by Hubert Henry Davies, a playwright who owed most of his fame, notably from *The Mollusc*, to Wyndham. Davies' work marked an interesting development from the fashionable milieu of Jones's Society drama, for he drew in miniature and (figuratively) in watercolors, providing a link between the cup-and-saucer comedies of Robertson forty years earlier and the calculated naturalism of Van Druten or Priestley twenty years later.

Wyndham's last years were saddened by an affliction of the memory which he inherited, but which was doubtless aggravated by the sheer drudgery imposed on the memories of Victorian actors; Ellen Terry suffered in much the same way. The effect was not of absent-mindedness but of inability to connect words and ideas. Thus Wyndham would hail a taxi and instruct the puzzled driver, "I forget the name of the theatre I want to go to, but it's the one named after me. *Take me there.*"[29] Mary Moore, who had married Wyndham after the death of his first wife in 1916, recounts an occasion when she sent the chauffeur to look for him in the Criterion, where he was found in "the Yacht," the office he had fitted up with full naval rig, turning over the scripts of all the plays he had bought but would never act.[30] It became necessary to spare him responsibility, and his son Howard took over much of the work of running the theatres. Howard Wyndham formed an admirable working partnership with Mary's son, Bronson Albery, which in the 1930's was to flower into one of London's leading producing managements.

Wyndham died in 1919 at the age of eighty-one. If his last years had been shadowed, his name was assured of honorable mention. So long as Wyndham's Theatre stands, his achievements will be recognized. Certainly he was lucky in reaching the zenith of his success during the 1890's, a period of great prosperity in the English theatre. Even the limitations of his acting were turned to advantage; debarred from the traditional "classical" repertory, he was able to perfect his particular brand of entertainment and build up a public that never deserted him. The small scale of his operations at the Criterion allowed him to put his theatrical empire on a firm financial basis—something that was sadly lacking in Irving's rule at the Lyceum or Tree's at Her Majesty's. This is abundantly demonstrated by the Register of Wills at Somerset House: Wyndham and Mary Moore each left fortunes of approximately £200,000. Irving left some £20,000.

In his book *Behind the Scenes*,[31] Cyril Maude, who learnt

---

[29] P. Hutchinson, *Masquerade*, p. 52.
[30] A. E. Matthews, *Matty* (London, 1952), p. 151.
[31] *Behind the Scenes with Cyril Maude* (London, 1927), p. 84.

his acting at the Criterion, recalls that Wyndham's motto was "Oh Lord! Keep my memory green," meaning, "Keep me young in ideas." As old age sapped his mental powers, this motto took on another and sadder meaning. But in the end the prayer was answered. His three theatres nightly receive their players and playgoers, continuing what he began. As the lights spell out "Wyndham's Theatre," as the faithful queues stretch round the corner till they can shake hands with the gallery-goers at the New Theatre, his wish is granted.

"Oh Lord! Keep my memory green."

Contributors

BERNARD BECKERMAN is Professor of Dramatic Arts and chairman of the Theatre Arts Division at Columbia University. Formerly chairman of Drama and Speech at Hofstra University, he served as Director of the Hofstra Shakespeare Festival from 1950 to 1965. In addition to articles on Shakespeare and dramatic theory and reviews of productions for *Shakespeare Quarterly,* he is the author of *Shakespeare at the Globe* (1962) and *Dynamics of Drama* (1970) and was co-editor of the New York Shakespeare Festival Series.

BARNARD HEWITT is professor and chairman of the Department of Theatre, University of Illinois, Urbana-Champaign. A past president and fellow of the American Educational Theatre Association, he was the first editor of *Educational Theatre Journal* and of the AETA Books of the Theatre. His publications include *The Art and Craft of Play Production* (1940); *Theatre U.S.A.* (1959); *History of the Theatre from 1800 to the Present* (1970); and, as co-author, *Play Production: Theory and Practice* (1949). He has taught also at the University of Colorado, Montana State University at Missoula, and Brooklyn College.

CHARLES BEECHER HOGAN is the author of *Shakespeare in the Theatre 1701-1800,* 2 vols. (1952-57), of *The London Stage, Part 5,* 3 vols. (1968), and of numerous articles on theatrical and literary subjects. He has been a member of the Yale English faculty since 1943, with the present title of Research Associate.

GEORGE ROWELL is Special Lecturer in Drama at the University of Bristol. He served as general editor of *Theatre Research* from 1961 to 1964 and is the author of *The Victorian Theatre* (1956). He has edited *Nineteenth Century Plays* (1953), *Late Victorian Plays* (1968), and *Victorian Dramatic Criticism* (1971). His work for the theatre includes the libretto of *Engaged!* adapted from W. S. Gilbert's play; a new version of *The Lyons Mail*, adapted from Charles Reade's play; and *Sixty Thousand Nights*, commissioned by the Bristol Old Vic to mark the Bicentenary of the Theatre Royal, Bristol.

CHARLES H. SHATTUCK is Professor of English at the University of Illinois, where he has taught in the departments of English and of Speech and Theatre since 1934. Director in the University Theatre from 1943 to 1963, he held the Henry Noble MacCracken Chair of English and was Director of the Experimental Theatre at Vassar College, 1948-49. He served as co-editor of *Accent, A Quarterly of New Literature* from 1940 to 1960. Guggenheim Fellow and Associate of the Center for Advanced Study during 1961-62, he held Folger Shakespeare Library Fellowships in 1959 and 1961 and is currently general editor of the Facsimile Promptbook Series of The Folger Library. His books include *Bulwer and Macready: A Chronicle of the Early Victorian Theatre* (1958); *William Charles Macready's KING JOHN* (1962); *Mr. Macready Produces AS YOU LIKE IT; a Prompt-book Study* (1963); *The Shakespeare Promptbooks: A Descriptive Catalogue* (1965); and *The Hamlet of Edwin Booth* (1969).